AWAKENING YOUR MENTAL
AND FINANCIAL WEALTH

Ali Shahraki

DEDICATION

I want to dedicate this book to my wife Kuldeep Shahraki, who has been with me throughout everything in life from a young age. She has looked after our 4 young kids while I worked, studied, and learnt or launched businesses and even went to university and had to study all night. She was even there when we were homeless.

Yes, she was there with me the whole time, watching us and our life changing day by day. Without her support, of being there and looking after our children, or even the time she had to go to work when I needed her help to support our family financially while I was learning, I would not be where I am today.

I also want to dedicate this book to our amazing children Kimia, Kian, Kiana, and Ariana for coping with me being busy, working, studying, and working on our future until I was free to spend my time with them.

Special thanks go to my Son Kian Shahraki, who is my business partner, and since the age of 5 he has been helping me in the marketing side of our business.

Also, I want to send a special thank you to my beautiful girls Kimia, Kiana, and Ariana for all their love and care support when my strength needed to be recharged to keep going and I needed a hug. I love their love letters to me; I find them everywhere I walk.

ACKNOWLEDGEMENTS

It has been an amazing journey from being homeless in 2002 to finally in January 2020 being able to work the hours I want and doing what I want. Also having the blessing of being able to choose what I do with my time, spending it with whoever I want and whenever I want, which is the true meaning of life…

I would not be here without some amazing people who helped me find my way and want to acknowledge.

I want to thank the one person who believed in me and signed me up for a higher education course I was looking for to go to university, after I passed my English and Math on the computer instead of writing by hand. Thank you for looking past my dyslexia.

I want to thank the people who helped our first-born daughter who was diagnosed with Autism, Cerebral Palsy and Global learning difficulties. The prognosis was that she would never walk or talk, that my daughter would never understand our feelings or be able to show me her love and care. Thank you to everyone who believed in her and helped her grow. It was a long journey, but she is now 18 years old and the most loving, caring young lady ever. She is the wisest person I ever met, and we have awesome conversations.

I also had many good people and mentors in my life journey, from whom I learned, some were in the darkest moment in my life.

I must say thank you to Ninyo the little but a wise Monk I met in Tibet when I went to dedicate my life to help humanity. He helped me to find my purpose by asking me the right questions.

I also thank the many great religious teachers I have met such as Dr Zakir the Islamic teacher in Malaysia, and Joel Osteen the great bible analyst, as I call him. I learnt a lot from Sadhguru the Indian Guru who has achieved inner peace within himself and also from life philosophers such as Omar Khayyam the Iranian philosopher or Dr Michael B. Beckwith the spiritual teacher. Thank you also to Tony Robbins and Richard Bandler for helping me to have a better understanding of what happened to me when I had my bike accident.

I would like to thank John Butcher the American millionaire for his wisdom about life planning. I send thanks to Greg Secker for his forex coaching.

I have to say thank you to all of my mentors even if I have not mentioned you by name, please accept my gratitude.

In different stages I have needed different kinds of help and thankfully the universe put some great people in my way. With their help I have grown and developed. There were so many, and I appreciate every single one of them.

Now I am on the mission to pass on the knowledge to others so I can help others change their life too, and that is why I created my Minds2Wealth program and all other related wealth creation programs that we offer at the school of trading UK.

I want to also thank my parents for being such an amazing mom and dad, thank you for teaching me so many lessons in life. I believe I am where I am today, because of your prayers.

You might not believe this, but every time before any big business meeting, I call my mom and ask for her prayers and blessings to be successful in what I am about to do. I feel like her blessings give me special powers, so I must thank my mom and dad for all their teachings, prayers, and blessing throughout my life.

I want to say thank you to Adrianne Carter, the face whisperer and special friend and mentor who did the edit on this book knowing I am dyslexic and needed help. Specially after my original publisher and editor took my money and left me half way, because he changed business. She even wrote the forward on this book which is my honour to have a multi award winning author and recognised industry expert to write a forward for my book. I was so determined to finish this book and I did it.

I am a people observer; I prefer to learn from the mistakes of others to save time. So, I observe and choose who I want to learn from. I learn from successful people who have achieved what I want, and I also learn what not to do from people's failures.

I have learnt a lot from other people mistakes and studying other people's actions so I want to thank everyone who taught me something by winning or failing in what they were doing so I could use the learning in my life and teach it to others too. As Isaac Newton put it, "If I have seen further, it is by standing on the shoulders of giants."

FOREWORD BY ADRIANNE CARTER THE FACE WHISPERER

I met Ali 5 years ago at a driving instructor conference.

I was invited to speak about one of my specialities', facial expressions, and emotions, at the conference for the audience's education and engagement.

There was an audience of a few hundred attendees, but one voice kept popping up from the audience with answers to my questions and with questions at the end of my presentation.... Any guesses who that might be?

After I finished my talk, the conference organiser approached me and told me that someone had offered to donate £1,000 to the conference charity if I and another speaker would do some coaching with the person's family.

We both of course said yes! And the rest as they say is history.

I got to know Ali and his family very well over the next few years and I'm proud to say we're friends.

I'm an expert on emotions, natural success, and behaviour. I've spent the last 20 years studying these subjects to the most in-depth level possible.

I'm often quoted in the media and have appeared on tv to commentate on the behaviour of celebrities or newsworthy people.

In the last 5 years, I've worked alongside Ali in various capacities and most recently as an expert on emotions and natural success in his Minds2Wealth coaching academy.

I've been able to see first-hand how passionate and supportive he is to all that come into contact with him.

The book is a revealing insight into how he changed his life and attitude after a serious bike accident and gives you a glimpse into his before and after mindset – fascinating!

He is succeeding in life both financially and in his relationships and he's a fantastic cheerleader for other people and helping them to succeed too.

He's poured his heart and soul into his this book, sharing his knowledge and personal experiences; both good and bad. After reading this book, you only will fail if you want to…

I urge all to read this book and put into practice the very practical elements that Ali has shared.

This isn't just about head knowledge, it's about very real strategies that work for personal and professional lives!

Ali delves into the nitty-gritty of how our minds work and how to get the most out of oneself so that the reader may do the same.

One of the key messages I've taken from this book is to change your mind, to change your attitude and you are guaranteed to change your life.

Picking up this book is the first step on your financial and mental success journey, and I know Ali and his Mind2Wealth programme will support you in as many ways as you need.

Good luck and enjoy the journey with Ali!

CONTENTS

INTRODUCTION

Hi, if you still do not know me, I am Ali Shahraki, a former Diamond Driving Examiner and UK DVSA Ordit registered Driving instructor trainer in Birmingham, who was born in Iran, but I've lived and been educated most of my life in the United Kingdom.

After many years of training, I became a wealth coach in 2019, and I was running many seminars around the country teaching people about wealth and life planning.

I stopped teaching people to drive back in January 2020 as I did not need to go to work for earnings anymore.

I am now a senior forex trader, stock market, Gold and Crypto market investing, mentor and investor. I am also a verified by account wealth creation coach with Level 4,5 and 6 in Coaching and an ICF registered Life coach, working with high performance and business people, helping them to overcome their mental obstacles in their success journey.

I run mentoring programs in our company, School of Trading UK, for people who are interested in investing and learning about stock market and forex.

I am a joint venturist with investors all around the world, helping them to invest and grow their money.

In 2010, April the 10th to be exact ... I had a bike crash which changed my life and made me to start a self-discovery journey to find myself and the path to success.

I made my way up from being homeless in 2002 to be financially free in 2020. You might be asking so why do you still work, invest or sell courses then? Well, the short answer is, making money is great. It helps me to help more causes close to my heart, plus you tell me, who doesn't want to make or have more money?

Well, if I make more money, then I invest more, and I make it grow even further, so then I be able to do more with it for others. It's fun to make money and see it grow further. Plus, it keeps me busy, as I am a highly active person.

The difference is now I get to choose when to work, how I work and how I spend my time during the day, instead of being forced to go to work. Before, as a driving instructor I had to work to earn to pay the bills, I had no choice.

Now I get to have the free time I always wanted because I am an investor, and I work online. Soon I will be able to finally start travelling the world, with my family when we know travelling is safe again after the Covid situation.

I have learnt a lot through the journey.

But it was not easy! … before 2010 I was Mr Angry and hated everything and everyone because of all my life events and my daughter's disabilities.

I lost my faith in everything even the existence of God and I was suffering from a deep depression. I simply did not have any hope in life anymore.

I was Mr Angry... and I always was blaming others for the pain and struggle in my life. This was Ali up to 2010 when I had my bike accident.

In that accident, I died for around 17 minutes. You can call it whatever you want, but the paramedic said there was no sign of life when they arrived 10 minutes after the crash and on his watch, I was out for 7 minutes before I came back.

I saw the event from outside my body. I had an out of body experience. That crash changed my life and the way I see life... it changed my life perspective. After that I made peace with my past and my death.

I was not scared of anything anymore from that point, because I had faced my death.

I nearly lost all my fears in life by facing my death. But there was and still is one fear in me, and that is something we call the fear of future regret.

It is the fear that when I am older, looking back at my life, and I see the things I did not try. It is the fear of not being able to say well done to myself for what I achieved in my life when I am at the end.

So, that is why I will try anything to improve my life and then try to influence others in a positive way too, and if it works then I will keep doing it.

At the same time, I also reflect on my life every day, week, month, year, and every 10 years to make sure I am doing everything I can to avoid that regret in the future.

I have never felt depressed or angry with any situations since my bike accident. After the crash, I went on a journey of learning for the last 11 years to find out what happened to me.

I've met many mentors, philosophers, and religious leaders. I even took training for a week in a temple of monks in Tibet to understand their views of the situation, and what happened to me.

Finally, the dots were connected, after I finished my 3 years life coaching training with Tony Robbins, studying with people such as Richard Bandler, Joel Austin, John Butcher, Dr Michael Bernard Beckwith and many more mentors that I've had in my journey of finding myself.

Now I live in the last hour of life because I do not know if I will have the next hour. I took being alive for granted, instead of appreciating it.

That experience made me love life and only do the things I love or make my heart happy. I learnt to forgive people quickly, and only live in a happy state, to create good memories for others. Before the crash, I was angry at the whole world, blaming everyone for my downfalls and decisions.

Now, I am a different person, and I live to serve and help others in the moment that we live. I live to create good memories for others, who I meet on my way through my journey of life. My mission is to affect people positively in my way.

Getting a second chance was enough for me to change my life. After 11 years of deep learning, I thought it was time to give back to people and fulfil my soul's need for contribution by helping others to even be happier like myself.

In the last 15 years of my research in to wealth and the 11 years of spiritual journey that I have experienced, I have interviewed many successful people, to find the secret to success, and I have turned my experience and my findings to a model that I called a Rebirth Model. I will be introducing my Model in this Book.

Also, I have created the Minds2Wealth program that teaches the Rebirth Model to help people following my path to a happier life. The Rebirth model is my foot print in this journey of life. The aim is to help people so they can create the road map they need to achieve what they want in life.

So, if you are lost, or have been stuck behind obstacles on your way in life or business, you should reach out to us. Maybe simply, you just need a lift to the next stage to improve your business, life, relationship, or health! If so, then you should go to:

www.Minds2Wealth.com

Or look for me Ali Shahraki on any social media to find me. Get in touch with me so we can help you in completing your journey the way you want it.

I look forward in helping you in this journey and to giving you the shift you need to the next stage.

Best regards

Ali Shahraki

CHAPTER 1

I Nearly Died but I Found My Life

It's not every single day that you wake up facing a near death experience but on this day I did. As I sit here writing my first book explaining to the readers what I went through on this day I am already receiving flashbacks of exactly what happened. As I sit here, I can feel the energy of the morning in question. I can see myself in a motion picture inside my head. It's already playing in my mind before I even explain to you exactly what happened on this incredible, yet painful, awakening of truth.

You see I nearly died on this day. I am ashamed to say that on that morning I had woken, and I had a terrible argument with my wife whom I love dearly. You see it had been a terribly dark time for me. Where everything seemed to be going against me. Everything seemed to be going wrong, nothing that I tried was working and I felt empty and already dead inside. I didn't know at the time, but this morning was going to ultimately shape and change the future and destiny of my life, but it did.

Many of you reading may have had a similar experience, a near death experience, an experience that has caused you such great harm inside your heart, your mind, and your soul that it has literally torn your life apart. And if you, like me, have experienced this level of pain and anguish then you will appreciate that one of two things can happen.

We will either stay trapped inside that moment like Groundhog Day, or you will change your life path extremely because these kinds of events are awakening moments we face.

But I urge to understand, if you want to make a change … it starts with you.

On this particular morning as I woke, I was in my normal, grumpy, arrogant, angry at the world mode. The emotions going through my mind were "everybody has it in for me" and when somebody spoke to me and asked me something my temper was very short, curt, angry, and aggressive. In fact, I hated myself and I hated my life. Even though there were people around me trying to help me I did everything to push them away and hurt them.

As I walked out of my family home, I knew exactly what I was doing, I knew that I was hurting my wife and my children. I knew that I was hurting my family and I knew that I was hurting myself, but I didn't care. I had enough of life's rejections, life's pain, of trying to move forward only to be slapped in the face, only to be knocked back. You see I thought that it was life holding me back but indeed it wasn't … it was me, myself, and I.

I got dressed in my full race leathers, and if anybody rides a bike, you will know when you jump on a bike and you are angry, what could happen. You are an accident waiting to happen on that bike. Your feelings and emotion are in charge of you in that moment and your logic is turned off. In that moment of being angry, you are an emotional decision maker which makes you dangerous.

And as I got on that bike with my wife having asked me to get something as small as a pair of shoes for our daughter, I was filled with rage. It caused so much rage that I remember the words that I was saying to my wife at that moment, and I knew what I was saying was wrong. I knew I was causing upset.

I knew that my wife just didn't know how to help me. And I knew that by climbing on my bike and turning on the engine and by revving it up on the drive I was saying "F" you I am going to drive out of here and I am going to speed like a maniac down the road. I was angry, I wanted attention, I was upset with the world and above all I wanted to hurt everybody around me. I even lost my faith because I saw God as source of all my problems. I was blaming God for giving me a disabled daughter. I blamed God for everything bad that was happening around me and around the world. So, I prayed and prayed to meet God to ask him why? Why is God so unfair? I was lost and disconnected from my Source and my creator. I was miserable and severely depressed. I prayed every day for my life to end...

I am ashamed of that day. I am ashamed to go back to that moment, I am ashamed to write the words that I am writing to you now. But if these words that I am writing to you now can help you, to stop you from making that same mistake, stop you from getting on that superbike or into that car, stop you having an argument with your wife, from causing pain to your family, your friends, your father, everyone around you then it is worth writing them.

If I can whisper words to you now don't get on that bike, don't be angry at the world, have the strength to look at yourself, because it is only inside yourself that you will find the answers to change. But I wasn't listening to anything or anyone and as I pressed the start button on the engine the sound of the bike just roared.

Vroom-vroom, vroom-vroom. I can hear the noise of the purring 600cc engine, a top speed of 120mph. I shamedly pulled off my drive and I drove down the road at full throttle. There was so much power going through the back wheel of the bike that the front wheel was lifting off the ground and actually at that moment I was insane, I was out of control and beyond any help.

Of course, I didn't even spare a thought for my wife and what she was thinking, standing there at the door seeing her husband tearing off on that superbike and that she was thinking "he's going to kill himself, my husband is going to kill himself" or about the pain or the worry at that moment that I caused her. As I look at myself now, I say to my wife "I love you, and I am so sorry for taking you through that pain … it wasn't me".

As I tore down the road my bike reached 50, 60, 70, 80, 100, 120 mph. I didn't even think about the people that I could have hurt and the harm that I could have caused by riding the bike like this. I didn't even think about the pain that I could have inflicted on others. I was purely a selfish and miserable and angry man but what happened next not only saved me, but it saved my family and it saved me from hurting anybody else…all for a pair of shoes.

As I tore down the road at 120mph I lost control of my superbike and it started to veer left and right and at that moment something happened that I couldn't believe. I had an out of body experience. My mind and my body came apart and I could see myself on my superbike I could see myself losing control. I was watching myself and at that moment the bike wobbled, it bucked and before I knew it the bike was tumbling away from me. I was sliding down the road in my leathers and at that moment everything went blank.

If you have been in a crash, you will understand that it is hard to remember, it is almost as if it is unreal, surreal what you are going through. In that moment of danger, that moment in which I could have died, I thought that I did.

When I woke up there were people screaming and coming around me, the ambulance had arrived, and I didn't know what had happened. I didn't know if I was dead or alive if I had gone to heaven or had gone to hell.

I didn't know what had happened, but it seems like I had an out of body experience. I saw myself on the bike still riding then I saw the whole crash from outside of my body. I was called out before my bike crashed. I didn't want to go back, but suddenly a voice said to me "Ali, it's not your time to go. Ali, it's not your time. We have work for you. You have work ahead. You are going to help people. You are going to change people. You've got a chance and from this moment we give you a second life and you can either choose to make a difference in that second life or not." That is when I found myself laying down on the floor with paramedics all over me.

And in that moment, everything changed.

After my outside body experience all my questions were answered. I went from a very confused, lost, and depressed man who lost hope completely, to someone who now knew his purpose, to someone who knew what he wants from life and most importantly what was his role in this earth. And trust me, that feeling is the most empowering feeling ever that a man can feel. Nothing is more powerful than a man or woman with a purpose to achieve something, because we go and get it. What stops people achieving something, is the fact they are not sure about their purpose in life or in that path that they are on, so they can't focus on winning it. Once someone is sure of their purpose on being somewhere or on any path, oh boy, nobody can stop that person from achieving what they want.

The man that I was, the way that I thought, the emotions and feelings that I had changed. I now knew that I had an opportunity to take on life and rebirth.

It was as if I had gone from Mr Angry to Mr Positive, Mr Doubtful to Mr Inspiring. I just didn't know how I was going to achieve the things that the voices said to me – that I was going to help people and that I was going to make a difference. The only message that I could remember very strongly after I came back, was to put others before yourself to be prosperous and happy in life.

I got up after coming back, looked above me in to the blue sky and said, Thank you.

Thank you, for answering my questions and showing me my path.

But the question was "How do I put others before myself?" Do I do charity work? Do I work as a Monk? What do I do? That is where I started to attend many courses and visiting many places and meeting many religious people or study their books to learn about their views on how to put others before myself. I really had to learn about myself and try to understand what happened to me in that accident, and why I felt so confident and positive after the accident. I had to find everything about myself first if I was going to achieve my purpose and my full potential.

I had to get to know me first before knowing others and helping them. I realised my problems and anger were all my own internal problems. As Tony Robbins put it in a conversation I had over the phone with him, when he attended our training course live session as a mystery guest, to answer questions and I was complaining about my wife and how I want her to change so I can love her again, and Tony turned the question on me and asked what about me? What do I need to change? He said something that day, I'll never forget...

He said get rich in your head before you can get rich in your pocket, love yourself first before you can love others and he was right...

Every day that passes by and I learn more about myself, the more I understand what he meant that day.

In my accident, I believed I was dead and that I was being sent back to life. The paramedics said that when they arrived, for 7 minutes there was no sign of life in me ...

I was technically dead for those seven minutes, and for around 10 minutes in between the accident and the ambulance arriving. I believe that I was literally given a second chance in life to step away from Mr Angry to be able to help other people achieve their life goals. Making life about others and not just me.

As you read through this book, I am going to take you through different stages of transformation in my life. In the first chapter it's important for you to understand...

I was at the lowest point in my life, but it was the best part of my life, because it has given me the opportunity to bring this book to you. It has given me the opportunity to go on an incredible journey of change, transformation, and personal growth, that has brought me to the point where I am today and becoming a fully published author.

As I wrote the rest of the chapters in my book and started to create a programme of transformation, you must understand that my transformation started the day that I nearly died, but the actual transformation didn't happen, until I understood who I had been before. I had to learn about myself in a deeper level so I could facilitate the change in me. I needed that understanding to help me to go from the person that I was, to the person that I am. I hope that as you are reading this book, you find the same inspiration as I did, understand the fact that you are not alone, and you can make a difference or change your path if you choose to do so.

My only hope is this – that you don't do what I did and drive 120mph, nearly kill yourself and hurt everybody you love in the process. I hope you enjoy reading the rest of the book. I am Ali Shahraki, and I am here to help you get your mental wealth aligned with your financial wealth. Good Luck.

CHAPTER 2

The Resistance to Change and How You Can Change It

That day, lying on the floor broken and technically dead I gave Mr Angry his marching orders and showed him the door. I chose to stop believing that I was a victim in life and to instead take up the challenge I was given and to help people instead. I am here to help you, if you too want to change things in your life, or if you just want to follow my story and be inspired about the possibility that life can be so much more.

Did I walk away from that accident a changed man? Absolutely. Did I walk away from that accident the man sitting here... the man who truly believes he can help other people? No, I had a lot of work to do first. The big transformation was yet to come. I needed to make massive changes and they were not always easy. I sometimes resisted these changes and had to overcome this resistance to change. I had to go through a long process of acceptance which was often painful and hard to do.

I spent time, money, and effort on personal development to become the man I am today. It has taken me years and over $540,000 (£400k GBP) worth of training to get here.

But I have some fantastic news for you and anyone else wishing to become a better person, the person that you were born to be. Change is possible.

And more good news is that you don't have to nearly die and spend a small fortune to get there. I believe that I have been through all of this to help others, others who like myself know deep down inside, if not on the surface, that they need to change. I went through all of this to make your journey easier and so that I could lead you through it. I know that it is hard even with a mentor, somebody who believes in you. I know that you will have to fight the resistance to change in order to reach your true potential. I know that it is natural to fear change because it takes us into the unknown. I know what it is to feel inadequate. But I also know that if Mr Angry can change so can you, and I have created a Model for people to follow my path if they choose too.

My journey was one of self-discovery as well as self-development because as I said in chapter one until I knew who I had been, who I was and who I wanted to be, I could not be the person I am today and be the person who can help others

… If I could not help myself first on my path, how could I help others?

Throughout this journey I had to answer many questions which I will in turn ask you the same question and expect you to start thinking about them and try to answer them. These are simple questions to ask … but difficult to answer. Some may take hours; others take weeks and others will always be a work in progress.

During my self-development I was fortunate to be able to work with some wonderful trainers and coaches including Tony Robbins, John Butcher and Dr Michael Beckwith who appeared in The Secret and who is part of Mindvalley.

One of the earliest questions I asked myself repeatedly is "Who am I?". I knew I wasn't Mr Angry anymore; I had left him dead in a motorbike accident. But I wasn't Mr Inspirational yet either. I could still be grumpy and defensive, even though I was working on myself. While I was asking this question, I learned from Dr Beckwith about the four life stages that us as human being go through and change our level or stage at any time if we choose.

The 4 life stages are:

Stage one is the Victim Mode, where you blame others for your failures and are not good at taking responsibility for mistakes and issues.

Stage two is the Manifestation Mode, when you are deep in to your mindset and self-development. This only happens if you are training your brain and working on your attitude to find the right mindset to be ready for the next stage of your life.

Stage three is the Being Mode, which is about simply being available to be the source of power, light and positive energy, and the positive vibration in the universe. Simply being there as an inspiration to others to follow the same path as you. Being someone that, because of the way you are, other people's lives get better and not worse.

Stage four, the last and the highest stage is the Conscious Living Mode, which Dr Beckwith call it the Godly level and that is the highest level of being a human. It is the time when you just do good things and follow good habits that you have learned without thinking about it or having guidance and others want to follow you. It is the level that you enjoy forgiving more than taking revenge on people, no matter what people have done to you. It's the level that you can't help it to always help others and be kind, no matter what people have done, or what you get in return. It's hard to achieve this level and requires a lot of mental growth and practices to achieve this level of being a human.

He speaks about these levels in this video:

https://www.youtube.com/watch?v=vg-D2DMFbhk

When I learned this, I realised that I was in victim mode. In fact, 90% of people are in victim mode and they don't even realise it.

When I rode off on my bike that day, I felt that the whole world was against me I felt that the whole universe hated me.

I realised after that this was not true. My wife was not against me, my family, my friends, all of these people were on my side. And life itself was not so bad either. I had a superbike and a home and a family. I realised that the universe had been giving back to me what I had been putting into it. I was giving negativity and in return I was getting negativity back.

I was not Mr Angry anymore, so I thought I was fixed, but I realised I was still in victim mode. I realised that I still felt I was at the mercy of life and circumstances. I needed to realise this before I could take responsibility for my own life and move onwards to manifestation mode. I didn't want to be a victim anymore.

So, the question was, how do I get out of this victim mode?

As I started to work on that question, I came up with the beginnings of what I have come to call the Rebirth Eye Model. I followed this method to tackle my anxiety and depression fully and finding out about myself. This is the model that helped me to achieve my deep inner peace and happiness in life and business. This is the model that helped me have the success mindset I have now, and I am about to share it with you. This is the model that I put together after many years of learning, research and interviewing successful people and used to help me to get to where I am today and beyond today in to infinity. I truly believe this model is the key to anyone success.

This is a wheel which I consider to be my wheel of happiness because, as I worked my way around it at different stages, I had to improve different areas of my thinking as I was going forward to be able to be the best of myself, and to be Happy Ali. And as I worked on each area, I was able to move from the Ali that survived that accident knowing I needed to help people to the Ali that has learned how to help people.

I needed to learn who I was first though. I realised that if I woke up and started arguing then my whole day was ruined. I hadn't believed that the universe works this way before but the more I learned the more I realised that I was in victim mode, in the victim stage of life. The definition of somebody in victim mode is somebody who looks for somebody else to blame. It's your fault I am not achieving this, it's your fault I can't do that. It's your fault I cannot lose weight. I realised that I was doing that.

I didn't want to be there anymore, but many people will stay there all their lives. These people do not take responsibility. I realise that I had to take full responsibility for the things in my life, for the circumstances in my life. I needed to stop blaming my dad for not having lots of money to give me to have a better life. I needed to take responsibility and to decide what am I going to do and what am I going to change?

I needed to change. I needed to learn how to be the best version of myself. I realise that I needed to get the right advice from the right people and follow a number of basic steps and make a number of changes in order to move forward and develop.

I went through many processes and found what worked and identified these steps.

1. The first step is to be aware there is a problem by increasing the self-awareness.

2. The second step is to accept the problem exist after identifying it.

3. The third step is to not ignore the existence of the problem and be ready to learn, change and improve the situation mentally

4. The fourth step is to draw an action plan to take action and improve the situation

5. The fifth step is to start self-development to develop your mind and to start to realise what is going on around you and that the universe is much bigger than what's inside your brain

In my case I found it difficult to do it alone, it would take a long time and I wanted it faster, so I reached out and asked for help. I hired many coaches to help me improve different area of my life. No, it was not cheap, and I was not rich back then, but it was something that I had to do to move up the stage. It was something that I was dying to achieve, because simply I was tired of my situation. I was tired of my miserable life, and how I felt about everything and everyone and how I thought everyone was against me. Later I found nobody was against me, it was me against myself and I was fighting myself from inside.

I even got, myself a brain coach to help me learn faster and teach me how to organise my head better to boost my learnings and accelerate my progress.

The key to success is, to not be afraid of reaching out and asking for help or working with mentors and coaches. That can accelerate your progress and help you save a lot of time in the long run, and time is something we cannot buy or get back when it's lost.

After going through above steps and completing my realisation stage it was time for a solution. As a solution, I created my Rebirth Eye model which are the steps I took in the last 10 years to fix the situation. It is the outcome of my many years of research, reading, learning, attending class and learning about myself.

1. The first step is raising your standard.

2. The second step is to make an effort in changing the story you tell yourself about yourself or your life or others.

3. The third step is to better yourself by knowing what you want and how you are going to achieve it, so you stop yourself from being confused.

4. The fourth step is to reset your belief so you can replace them with good and correct beliefs that benefits you long term.

5. The fifth step is that you need to inspire yourself. What goes in is exactly what comes out. You can do this by meditation, listening to motivational speakers, reading the right books.

6. The sixth step is to train yourself in making good decisions and that comes by solving people problems and serving others. As Zig Ziglar said it once, 'solve enough people problems and you will be financially free soon.'

7. Finally, the seventh step is to hold and to give it 100% by having the determination to achieve.

This is how my Rebirth Eye model was formed.

When I started to develop myself, I was taking course after course trying to find answers. I felt for many years that I have taken many wrong courses. People asked why the courses were wrong, was it the content or the trainer? But I answered that, it was me. I had no direction, and if I had known where I wanted to go then I would have arrived where I am now more quickly!

I believe that my journey allowed me to grow and to learn things that I can pass on to others, to help others, but you don't need to wander aimlessly. The journey is long enough if you know the route. So, ask yourself. Where do I want to go? What do I want to do? What do I want to achieve? Why am I going on this journey?

And the most important question of all…

How am I going to achieve it? What plan do I have for my journey?

My journey was one of spiritual development, but also a journey of mental transformation.

I have designed a training programme called Minds2Wealth Program to help people go through this transformation, subject to them wanting to execute and to keep learning about themselves. It is based on my Rebirth Eye Model, and I support members as they make the journey in the group coaching environment. Many of you will progress through the levels and achieve higher levels of understanding. For those that make progress through the levels of learning there is an incredible opportunity to work with Minds2Wealth as a Certified coach, instructor, or trainer.

I joined the courses to work on myself. In the process I became a coach too. I suddenly looked around myself and I thought that everybody had changed. I said this to my wife one day, but she said, we haven't changed, but you have changed a lot, your attitude is totally different to few years back. I was very proud to hear all of that from my wife. I had to go through the transformation myself first instead of expecting others to do it and change first. I had to be the first to change my world and people's perspective, so then I could help others. The battle always starts within you, and if you cannot win the internal battle, you never will win the external battle, and you will never be able to help others with your love and care. By doing it myself and winning the internal battle I was facing for years, suddenly everything changed, and I could see this from the feedback from people.

You will remember from the first chapter that after my accident I knew I needed to change so I looked for ways to transform myself. I went on a journey of self-development and trying to find myself to transform into the person I am today. Over those years since 2010 I have come across many great leaders and mentors. The real mentors helped me to connect all these dots in my journey.

I learnt, to love others it is important that I love myself first. Caring and loving others always start with self-love. You only can love and care for others if you are full of love and care inside you, and that means you have so much love for yourself that now you can share it with others. Otherwise, you are just a broken jug, empty of love which you are just pretending to love and care for others for some reasons.

I travelled and I went to meet many religious people and philosophers, because I believed that perhaps my problem was because I had lost my faith and the fact that I didn't have any belief anymore. I wasn't connected to the higher being and I was thinking that I was the only one that was making all the decisions in my journey, I thought everything was in my hand. It was a lonely feeling, I just wanted to know what happened to me in my bike accident and what it meant for my journey.

The journey was quite a costly and time-consuming journey. I had to go to different places, pay for travel and hotels and not go to work. Just this part of the journey cost me over $30,000.

It cost me $5000-$6000 just to go to Tibet for two weeks to meet a monk. That is where I found I did not have the healing power of the monk, so it was useless of me trying to be a monk. It was there where I found that I was born to make money and use the power of making money to help charities more so they can spread their help to more less fortunate people around the world. In that way I could serve the people too and share the blessings of having a positive impact on people lives. It was there where I stopped hating money and I realised what was my role in this world. It was there where I found how I should help and put others before myself. I only had just one coaching session with that monk, and he saw through me deeply. He said "Ali, why don't you go and make money"? I said to him I don't want to make money, because I hate money and I believe it is the root of all evil. He helped me to change my mind thermometer; That was the place where I stopped believing money was dirty. He made me realise how the intention and how money was used, was the important part and it would determine if the money was seen as bad or good. The way money was used was important and how it was impacting the world.

I realised that I could make money and still be a nice person. I could then use the money as a tool to help people and support charities, which is what I do now. Twenty-five percent of my wages goes to help homeless people because I don't want other people to suffer the pain that I had. Recently I have created a Club, called FGC Club (Financial Growth Club) which I give access to all my financial education at affordable prices. The aim is to make financial education affordable for any average person. Also, all the profits go directly to Homeless charities or buying gifts for less fortunate kids. That has created a win/win situation for my inner peace because I benefit average people with my financial knowledge so they can design their future the way they want and not have to struggle anymore, plus we can feed more homeless people. I was homeless myself in 2002 and I know how it feels to be hungry, looking in the bin for food, so I try my best to help as many people as possible. I realised that by making money I can actually help more people than by walking around the streets and trying to comfort people with the healing power I did not have.

I now believe that money is a good tool to help other people, but it took a long time to be able to reset that in my mind. It was a long journey and I spoke to a lot of people like Joel

Austin, Tony Robbins and Richard Bandler. I have taken many NLP courses, courses with Andy Harrington where I did iron bending, wood breaking. I have even done helicopter jumping to overcome my fear.

It finally came to the point where I joined Tony Robbins course to become an ICF accredited life coach … not to get the qualification but to try to connect all of these dots because everybody was giving me different information and until I didn't know what was what, I could not make sense of it all.

Doing this course, in three years of learning about life coaching, I had to do lessons, assignments and live sessions in front of masters, trying to help people reset their mind while I was in the UK, and they were in the USA. I had to do them at 2am in the morning and I had to stay awake in order to be able to do all of the training. I found myself sleeping for only two hours a night because most of my mentors were in America. To be able to work with them and talk with them I had to stay awake at night and sleep during the day.

This did not include my journey in forex, this was just my self-development; working on myself to fix what was broken inside me and to come to the belief that I can have money and also be a good person.

I have studied with Dr Michael Beckwith. I spent a week with John Butcher creating my life plan. I studied with Jim Quick to learn how to read more quickly so that I could read more books. All of this and more I learned to become the Ali that I am today.

You see nobody ever tells you the hardship they went through to achieve what they achieved, because they want to look cool. You see, how extreme and seriously you take your mental health and mental strengths, depends on where you want to be and how you want your life to be in the future. An awesome life requires awesome strong mental health because to have an awesome life you must solve more problems and be more resourceful and not resourceless. To solve more problems and to be resourceful, you need strong mental health and a good decision-making mind.

This journey was like Ali's Adventures in Wonderland, and if someone had asked me, I might have responded much like Alice did to the Cheshire Cat:

'Would you tell me, please, which way I ought to go from here?'

'That depends a good deal on where you want to get to,' said the Cat.

'I don't much care where--' said Alice.

'Then it doesn't matter which way you go,'

said the Cat.

'--so long as I get SOMEWHERE,' Alice added as an explanation.

'Oh, you're sure to do that,' said the Cat, 'if you only walk long enough.'

Alice's Adventures in Wonderland by Lewis Carroll

But, there was one big difference between my adventure compared to Alice. The difference was, I did not want to end up just anywhere. I wanted to end up where I wanted to be. I wanted to design my own future and not just leaving it to luck. So, I had to do something different to everyone who was walking the same path and was getting the same result. I had to start looking at other people results, specially the one who achieved the results I wanted before me and left a foot print and that is why I have added having a role model in Re birth eye model in the section of better yourself. Having a role model would have lighten up my road and path to where I wanted to be. That is why at the start of my journey I started looking at 50 of my favourite successful people I wanted to use as my role model because I loved their life results, and I wanted my life to be like them. I realised whatever I wanted, was achieved before me by someone and all I had to do was to find the best model and use their journey as my model to be guided close to where they ended up. That was a miracle finding, because I did not need to invent the path, all I had to do was to follow someone who has gone through and got to the end results that I want.

I would suggest to you ask yourself "Where do I want to go?" then find someone who is gone there. Their journey can help you massively and you are lucky if they would be willing to mentor you in your journey to make your journey shorter and less painful.

You must not underestimate the level of commitment it takes to make this kind of transformation. When going through this journey everybody comes to a time when they are going to break, when they are going to snap, where they are going to doubt, where they are going to want to give up. And 85-95% of people will turn back at this point saying it's not working, it's not worth it, it's not happening quick enough, I don't feel any different.

I ploughed on though and suddenly all of the things I had studied, the programmes I had written in the past and all of the learning that had seemed irrelevant suddenly fell into place like the pieces of a jigsaw puzzle. It all started to make sense.

I had to stay committed though and so will you. Never underestimate at any time that this is just a course where you will take the red pill, or the blue pill and your life will be fixed. The only reason that I am the CEO of Minds2Wealth is that I have lived it, breathed it, endured it and I am still enduring it now as I write this book to bring this birth elephant to life.

All of my life has come to this moment of realisation that actually I am teaching people to enjoy wealth now by teaching foreign exchange and investing in different markets to help people to have more free times doing what they want, but actually I realise that I now know my purpose. I now know where I am going, but the time where I didn't know, where I was not quite sure which direction I was going and when I was asking myself am I going to be a coach or a teacher, am I going to be in wealth and investing or be a social media expert or be the best driving instructor or and or...

After all, I had many skills and attended many courses to be the master of everything as they teach you in schools and expect you to be master of all skills and subjects. I felt like I had to use them all separately. The clarity came to me when my wife sat me down and asked, who are you? Because when people ask me what your husband job is, I don't know what to tell them and she was right. I was focusing on too much and that is why I was not achieving the results I wanted from none of my skills. That is why I had to re write my mission for myself to make it more focused and I had to find out at the deeper level what I wanted from my life. That is why you see the mission in better yourself section of the Rebirth Eye model. I had to change my purpose and goals to adjust them properly a few times in my journey, but I did not need to forget my skills. I realised all the courses and skills that I had was coming together under something bigger to serve others in a bigger way...

Every single one of these developments has formed part of the jigsaw in my Minds2Wealth blueprint which I will be rolling out after the publication of this book.

This takes patience, commitment, and determination to hang on at all costs because if you can, you will have truly shifted the way that you think, act, and feel in your life in order to execute your mind and your wealth to where you are in a beautiful position for you, your business and your family. Whatever it is that you desire to have, you have to hang on.

Finding your why!

So, how can you overcome the obstacles on your way in your journey? How can you stay motivated to keep going? Well, that starts from the beginning of the journey and before you even start the first step. You have to find your why, and why you want to change your situation? why do you want to go on this journey of change?

I like to use a method which helps people to dig deeply into their psyche and to find the deep routed 'why'. If your why is to just serve yourself and buy more cars or houses, you never can use that 'why' to help you overcome obstacles. The 'why' which motivates you overcome obstacles in your journey is 'why' which is beyond just serving you. It becomes incredibly altruistic and connected to the higher being. The true why is connected to your soul and achieving it, is truly satisfying and that is why it keeps you going.

At the end of the day, us humans, love to do things to be loved. Sometimes, we are already loved, but we don't see it, so we try to prove to others, they should love us, while they already do. A good example is the love of your wife or children. You feel like you need to do something, so they love you, but they already love you. To them you are already a superhero, just open your eyes and see it.

To complete this transformation, you will need:

Persistence

Determination

Will to achieve

Understanding that change takes time

To be open to new ideas

Open to learning

The ability to accept that some of the skills we do not have yet but will have in the future

Constant development

Constant state of change

Constant state of openness

Constant state of acceptance

And patience that the seeds you are sowing now you cannot harvest now.

There is a story about the Chinese Bamboo Tree which I will tell you about it now. During my journey of change many times I felt despondent because of my progress. It felt that despite my efforts nothing was changing and that all my efforts have been fruitless. Every time I felt that way and I spoke to my mentor at the time, they always told me about the Chinese Bamboo Tree. I heard it several time in my journey to keep me going and understanding the fact that change requires time.

The story goes, the seed of the Chinese Bamboo is so hard that when it is planted nothing at first happens. The farmer must water it and protect it. After the first year no shoot shows, after the second and third still nothing shows even after the fourth nothing will show above the ground. In the fifth year finally, a shoot emerges. It grows up to three feet a day until in six weeks it is 90 feet tall. My mentors always asked: "How long did it take the bamboo to grow?"

"Six weeks," I replied the first time I heard the story, while I was very confused. "That is your mistake," replied my mentor. "It took five years. The seed needed time to sprout, to become strong and to create a firm foundation. The same is true of you. You must tend to your growth as the farmer did the seed. You must have faith that under the surface the foundation is growing and strengthening the same as the farmer had faith in the bamboo seed. If the farmer had not watered the seed, it wouldn't have grown."

You can see this story on YouTube:

https://www.youtube.com/watch?v=hLJFx_b2A2k

Change isn't easy and is really an ongoing process, but it is worthwhile. Life gets easier when we are more open, less defensive, less angry, and less in denial. People respond better to us; we achieve more, we feel more positive and get more positive results.

Do you remember that in the first chapter I said that life was giving back what I was putting in? I was putting in anger, suspicion, intolerance, and I was closed off. Now I have changed my mindset, life still gives me what I put in. The difference is that I am putting in kindness, compassion, understanding and openness. When we are open in this way some beautiful things start to happen.

You must understand that you have been given the choice, we are the only creatures on the planet who have the choice to wake up and think how life is going to be for us. If You are not where you want to be right now, it is because of the decisions you have made in your past, the decisions that shaped your future and now.

And if you are willing to take full responsibility then you are ready to change your future because now you are in the past of your future, and you can shape your future the way you want it. Your next 10 years does not have to be the same as your past 10 years, all it takes is a decision to have a different future. It is all down to if you take responsibility and if you are willing to learn, change and get prepared for a different future. This sounds tough and harsh, but it is the truth. You have to take full responsibility for everything in your life. You cannot change somebody else's views or behaviour. You can advise, teach, nurture, encourage or even plead, rant or punish but only they can choose to comply. You have control over the way **you** respond to a situation. That is why you only ever change your future if you really want to change it, no matter what everyone said.

My accident had a profound effect on my life!

What happens in your past shapes you. My accident had a profound effect not only on me but on those around me. It allowed me to become a better person. A person I am proud to be. Sure, I am not perfect, and I don't always make the best decisions, but I strive to be the best version of me.

If we take responsibility for our life and the things that have happened for us, we will arrive at the desired destination at the end, and not just at any destination. It will be the destination we imagined, and we always wanted.

My purpose it to help others, to give hope to other people, to tell people Santa Claus is real! This kind of hope is so important to people that even as adults if you say that Santa is not real some people become angry. In some people's childhood the only hope they had was in Santa … because they had no love from people.

We need hope … tell yourself Santa is real, and the tooth fairy is real, the Easter bunny is real. These are all just symbols of hope. We all need a symbol of hope. It is easy to kill hope, but my job is to make sure that the symbol of hope is high up, that the flag of hope is flying high, to make sure that people have hope. A symbol of hope is an anchor, to put into the ground to secure you. It is a symbol of your beliefs, and you need to change your belief. It is the symbol of you telling yourself the good things are coming so you look forwards to it or life become very miserable. We are now in December, and I love

December, because every afternoon, well most days at least, I put my Santa suit on and drive around with my kids in my car with Christmas songs playing the whole time. You should see how we make other people dance and happy, even if it is for a few moments. You might say, well you are not Christian. I say to you, being happy don't understand or need any reason or religion.

I celebrate with all faiths and religions holidays…

Did you ask why? Because they are always a good reason to be happy for any reason…

Change your belief. Believe that you can and that you will. Believe that you have all you need to succeed or will have all you need to succeed. Read the biographies and autobiographies of successful people, listen to inspirational leaders, watch inspirational films. Fill yourself with hope for the future and the belief that it is the future that you will achieve.

A famous Henry Ford quote is "Whether you think you can, or you think you can't – you're right," emphasizes how much attitude determines success or failure. He might have equally changed the word think for the word believe

It is all about the belief more than anything else…

What are your beliefs? You will remember that I believed that money was the route of all evil. I went all the way to Tibet and needed to be told by a monk that this was not true, and that money is an incredible tool for good in the right hands. All I needed to do is to make money and get it into the hands of these people to be able to help many more people than I could ever help physically with my one body, one pair of hands and 24 hours in a day.

Do you have beliefs that are not serving your purpose? Not earning money meant I was helping fewer people. This went against my purpose. What are your beliefs? Are they serving your purpose? If not, then you need to change them. I believed that every rich person in the world became rich by stealing from other people.

This stopped me from becoming rich. I believed that maybe my sister was going to hate me if I had more money than her. I had to change this. I had to realise that she would be happy if I had money to help her and support her. I believed that my mum would think I was a different person if I had money but then I realised that she would love it if I were to hire an aeroplane and take her somewhere. I needed to change my vision.

What is your vision? How are you looking at life? Have you changed your channel? If you haven't changed your channel, don't you think it's time for it? Aren't you tired of the vision you had from before? Because whatever your vision is, whatever beliefs you have, something is not serving you. Something is holding you back. How do I know? Because if you had all of the beliefs and the vision that would serve your purpose and make you the best of you that you could be, then you would already be there. If your current beliefs and vision were the best, the most ideal that they could be then the chances are you would not be reading this book.

I ask myself these questions every week because I am a work in progress. I am a much better Ali than I was … but am I the best version of myself? I am the best version of myself that I can be now and the best version of myself is the one that is constantly striving to be better.

Another of the beliefs I had was that people should each bring 50% to a relationship. This was not serving me. I realised that I thought my wife should fetch me tea. I became resentful because I felt that she was not giving her half of the relationship. She maybe felt the same. It probably didn't occur to her to make me tea because she was busy and didn't notice time going by. I realised that giving half belief was not helping me.

I realised that I needed to give 100%. When I started to give 100%, I noticed my wife also gave 100%. Maybe she gave 100% all along but because I gave only 50%, I felt that she wasn't. I changed my vision and my relationship changed. We need to have that vision of the future. Because change is frightening. Change is scary for us as people because we don't know what it will look like. This is why it is so important to have that clear vision of the future that we desire because otherwise we will not know where we are going and that is frightening. Have you changed your visions yet?

If you don't know what you want from life, then you will find it difficult to change. I was confused. I woke up every morning thinking "what am I going to do now?" I had no plan. I was jumping from branch to branch doing this and that comparing myself to this person and that person.

And none of it was helpful. I had to write down my vision for the future. This is what I want in the next ten years, this is what I want in the next 20 years, this is what I want in the next 90 years. My son said to me you won't be around in 90 years, and I said I wrote that for you so that you know what I would have done if I was here.

As we go through these changes and as we move through this transformation, as we go through this resistance to really accepting and embracing this change one of the things that I believe is important is understanding people.

Understanding the way that they think, not just the way that you think and what your preferences and values are, if you can understand other people, you are never then judging someone else on your values compared to what their values are. As men and women and children we all have different values, and we think in different ways.

As Mother Teresa says:

'If you judge people, you have no time to love them'

- Mother Teresa

When I was at university, we had a lecturer who had a lot of knowledge. He would take his heart apart for us teaching us everything he knew. But everybody would laugh at him and throw paper at him, all because he was wearing a childish pink watch. The year ended and all of us passed, he gave us all good grades, he was a very good man.

I went to him, and I said to him why do you make yourself look like a clown? This was me then, judging people, not understanding people. I have stopped doing this now I have stopped asking why people are doing something. This is their why and not my why and that is something I learnt from the answers I was given in my outside body experience. It is not my responsibility to ask why you are doing something. I am only responsible to ask my own why. I am only allowed to ask, why am I doing that?

So, I asked my lecturer why are you wearing that watch? Everyone is laughing at you. He said son, I had a daughter, and she was seven years old when she died because of leukaemia. This is the last thing I have from her. I was shocked. I said seriously.

He said, this watch is not even working but when I have this watch on my wrist, I feel that she is with me. It gives me a strength; without this watch I cannot wake up in the morning. People on this course thought that this guy could not afford to go and buy a watch. I said I am sorry, because I was one of them thinking what is wrong with this guy? I didn't understand his why.

We cannot always understand other people's why, but it helps us to understand other people's personalities. If you know how other people think you are not always thinking about your own thoughts and values, you can think about somebody else, and this makes you a stronger person.

To help you I have created a questionnaire…. go to my website and fill it out.

Finally, let me tell you that this book is going to ask you questions, it will create questions within you, and these will lead to still further questions but there are three questions which I am going to ask you at the end of every chapter. This is because as you go through my book, you will experience growth and change and as you do your answers to these questions you may grow and change too.

I took you to Wonderland earlier and now I will take you back there and much as the caterpillar asked Alice, I, Ali ask you:

Who are You?

What do you want from life?

I also ask:

Why do you want that?

CHAPTER 3

It Was My Ugly Other Twin Not Me

Inside each of us there is a positive energy and a negative energy. Inside each of us there is opportunity and there is lack of opportunity. Inside each of us there is success and there is failure.

In this chapter I am going to share with you a story that I have come across called The Good Wolf and the Bad Wolf. Only you can decide which wolf to feed. But before I tell you this story, let me talk to you about the three questions that I left you with at the end of the last chapter. If, as I suspect some of you will have done, you swept past them onto this next chapter then stop reading, get a pen and paper and put down three answers, one to each of the questions. I need you to think about these questions before you move on.

They sounds very simple; however, they are perhaps three of the most important and profound questions that you are ever going to hear.

Let me repeat them:

Who are you?

What do you want from life?

Why do you want that?

I have found through my own experience, my own lessons, of spending many thousands of pounds of investment in personal development that these are the most important questions that could be asked of anyone who is looking to make a change in terms of mindset and/or of achieving a greater level of success within their wealth.

Many people when you ask these three direct questions don't know the answers. Some of you do.

However, if you are somebody that is still pondering and still thinking about "Who am I", "What do I want in my life and my business?" and "Why do I want that?" you're not alone. We see people at the fork in their life every day. It is normal to feel confused, but remember you have a choice to stay confused all your life or get help and find your way. Again, the choice is yours, just remember you have a choice. You can choose to be happy every day or be miserable all your life. You can choose to stay confused and lost or come to Minds2Wealth and let us help you find the way. I have done it for me, I can do it for you too.

It is essential that you have an answer because when you are given an opportunity, and you don't know where you want to go, how are you going to choose a direction?

I want to tell you about the wolf story, the story that defines the meaning of choice and direction…

We are all facing the biggest challenge, more than any creature on the planet, and that is the power of making decisions. We are the only creature that has been given the power of making decisions. We can make decision to be bad or good, positive, or negative, but a goose or a Dog cannot choose how they feel, what they do or what they should do. That is not to say they don't have feelings, but their destiny has been written for them in their DNA and they can't change it because they cannot choose what they are doing. It is easy to say that, but there are a lot of emotional control and other elements in us as human beings have direct effects on making those decisions.

There is a story that goes that a Native American lady is teaching her grandchild because he is finding it difficult to decide about life, to decide about which way to go and what to do and what kind of person he wants to be in the future. She tells him that we all have two wolves inside of us - the bad wolf and good wolf. The wolves are always there fighting to try to take charge. The bad wolf is evil —he is anger, envy, sorrow, regret, greed, arrogance, self-pity, guilt, resentment, inferiority, lies, false pride, superiority, and ego she explained. The other is the good wolf — he is joy, peace, love, serenity, humility, kindness, benevolence, empathy, generosity, truth, compassion, and faith.

The same fight is going on inside you — and inside every other person too.

The grandson thought about it for a minute and asked, "Which wolf will win?" Then she simply replied. "The one you feed."

https://www.youtube.com/watch?v=__cdpyF5nLk

And you know, the more you feed the bad wolf, the more the bad wolf grows, and the more you feed the good wolf the more the good wolf grows. And for the last 15 years I've been a starving the bad wolf inside. And I've been feeding the good Wolf, you know, to try to be more in the light instead of being more in the dark. Life is constantly about improving, mentorship and learning from experiences.

When we feed the good wolf, we are in alignment, and we are more aligned with our values and heading to where we want to be. When we feed the bad wolf, we fall in the trap of victimhood which gets us in to the crazy 8 cycle of depression. The crazy 8 shape cycle of depression is when we go from one side of the cycle to another side, and we keep repeating the cycles without knowing how to get out of it. That is where we need a breakthrough moment to break out of the crazy 8 cycle. The cycle usually goes from feeling victim then upset to angry then depressed and back again in to the victim mode and we keep repeating the cycle. The only way out is to do something to interrupt the cycle.

That is why they say, the beast never dies inside … it is always there … we constantly must feed the good wolf.

But how do you feed the good wolf? By doing good deeds, by helping other people, by adding love to everything. Also, by developing yourself, developing your mind.

One of the important things to understand about the good wolf and the bad wolf is not just what to feed them, but who you are.

And I didn't know who I was…

I was a very confused man, because for years I was feeding the bad wolf and I was drawn in the stories I was feeding the bad wolf to stay in the victim mode of life. I feared change.

I created my Rebirth Eye Model to help you, but it cannot help you until you are ready to change. I want to help you and I am here for you.

The choice is yours but move forward if you are honestly ready to make a change and open to look inside yourself and open to criticise things about your current belief and behaviour. You can ask your friends and family, to say, "listen, I'm going through a transition, and I need your honest help". And I did this myself. I asked people what they thought about me. I asked people at my university what they thought about me.

They answered that everybody just let me get away with whatever I wanted to do and when I asked them why they said because Ali if we ever said to you "don't do that" you would turn into Mr Angry. You would have a go at us, you would make us feel bad so we ended up not even being bothered to question you because we knew what would happen. You would be defensive; you wouldn't be open.

And I wasn't. I hurt myself and my family for many years.

I work hard on myself, even spent a week with the multimillionaire John Butcher producing my life plan which is 178 pages. I wanted to know how he manages his life because he has balance. I really respect him because he accepts other people's opinions and is down to earth so you feel you can talk to him like any other person.

I have spent around 10- or 11-years investing time and money in my self-development. I did the Robbins Madanes course From Tony's academy to learn how to become a life coach, because I was doing forex trading and I kept losing money. I realised the reason I was losing money was because I had the wrong personality. I was making wrong decisions because I was thinking wrong. I had to learn that my environment affects me, my thoughts affect me, and all of that and everything else affects my decision-making process.

I must have a ritual, a special ritual to be able to make decisions. I don't just sit down and assess the market just like that. I must be very calm, very relaxed, no arguments. All of this affects your decision making.

At first, I would not accept that this was the problem. I would lay blame … I would say this is a scam, that is a scam … everything is a scam. I couldn't trust anyone because I couldn't trust myself.

I want you to realise the fact, as human beings, we all have that inner chatter that tries to put us off from taking action and creates doubts in us to stay put, to keep us safe. You should understand that your mind could be playing tricks on you, but you should know that you have the power to control your mind and that inner chatter to stay in charge of making decisions.

Rebirth and accepting change

The rebirth is a massive shift inside of yourself that makes you feel like an entirely new person, but it all starts from accepting that change is needed. It is as if you've got the sudden ability to be able to go back and change everything we don't like in our lives. The things that hurt us. The things that have shaped us ultimately from childhood. Now, I don't mean that you would change these things, but that you can look at them in a whole different light, in a whole new way that no longer causes you pain.

I wouldn't want to go back and change anything at all in my life. Why? Because it is my past that brought me to this position, to the place where I was able to be reborn. I no longer feel that the things in my life happened **to me** – no, they happened **for me**. Take my accident, it happened for me to help create the person I now am. The person whose mission it is to help other people achieve the same awakening. I am completely comfortable. I feed the good wolf every single day and I accept my past as a journey of betterment. And that is what I want to help you achieve for yourself. I am grateful for everything that comes my way even my sickness. In 2021 I fought Covid 3 times, and I won against Omicron once too, even though I was vaccinated after the first time I got it. Now again today I tested positive for the 4th time in January 2022 as I am editing this book. So basically, most of my time in 2021 I was sick, and I see myself as a survivor and fighter of Covid-19.

The sickness made me want to stay in bed most of the time. I had a choice to be depressed and give in to sickness and stay behind in life and business or mentally win it first and keep fighting it strong and get on with my life. I choose to win it mentally and continue with my life and started writing my book. I am so grateful for everything, because sometimes God has to push us to stop and look. So, when I got sick, I had time to sit, look back and write this book to create a foot print for people after me. I went from being homeless in 2002 and an incredibly angry man to be living on passive income from 2020 and achieving all my financial goals and be a different happy and grateful man. In 2020 I just decided to stop smoking after 20 years. That day I stopped with no help or replacement and never touched smoking again to the point now I hate it and cannot stand the smell of it at all. I saved our marriage from the edge of getting divorced after 21 years of being together by changing my own mindset.

I decided to home educate my son from the age of twelve because he was getting bullied most of his school time. The bullying was making him cry every day, he was not doing well in any of the school subjects. Being bullied had not just affected him mentally but also, he was affected physically. He looked like a five-year-old in his age of twelve, but only one year of home schooling everything changed, at the age of thirteen he sold over $13000 on the internet using his affiliate marketing knowledge he was learning from his home education. Now sixteen, he has his own internet marketing business, making sales funnels, helping businesses to move online and working on metaverse development. He also runs his own internet marketing courses and has his own students attending his teachings. Totally different result from what his head teacher predicted for him the day I took him out of school, and he shouted, this boy never achieves anything in his life, and I shouted, 'you will see' and walkout of school with him...

So, people keep asking me how do I do it? And I say, by achieving breakthrough moments. By first believing in it and achieving the belief in my mind that I can do it and it is possible, then nurture my beliefs until I see results in whatever I wanted to see results. So, now this book and Mind2wealth program is how I do it and I hope it will help others to do it too and achieve everything they want in their life. Achieving what you want, requires specific mindset and strength. Some of us are born with that mental strength, but some of us like me, must train themselves in it to achieve the mental strength which is needed for the journey of life and success.

Feed the Good wolf within you so you be able to forgive and let go fast!

Trust me, forgiving saves a lot of time and energy from being upset and holding on to bad feelings for days. I have a thirty second rules for forgiving. I allow myself to be upset from a situation but only for 30 seconds, then I have to forgive or apologise to end that situation to move on.

The reason is because of my near-death experience with my bike accident. Since then, I do not take life for granted anymore, because I do not know how long I have left. So, I live in the last hour of life. I always ask myself, if I only have one hour left, would I spend it all on being upset? Of course not!

I choose to take responsibility instead of waiting for the other party. Usually, I forgive or apologise to free us both. Having that thirty second rules meant, I have managed to live a happy state all the time, which is productive and creative mode of being human. As you know, all life progresses, and good decisions are happening while you are in productive and creative mode. I love to make progress, don't you?

So, remember to forgive others fast for you, not the other person so you can live free faster and longer.

By feeding the good wolf you will have the ability to let go and forgive faster. Whatever way you want to define that – letting go of your bad trash, letting go of your bad habits, letting go of your bad thoughts and feelings, letting go of the bad situations.

Remember as Master Oogway said:

Yesterday is history,

tomorrow is a mystery

but today is a gift

which is why it is called the present.

-Oogway

Ladies and gentlemen let me share with you now, something that has taken me ten years of sacrifice, ten years of self-development, ten years of feeding my good Ali Shahraki wolf to create. Let me share with you my Rebirth Eye model.

In this chapter you will now realise that we have been looking at the "better yourself" module of my course. Feeding the good wolf is one of the ways to better yourself but there are more.

There are five areas to address in this module:

1. Your mind where we cut the weeds and get rid of blockages.

2. Strengthen your body.

3. Finding your mission.

4. Finding a role model.

5. Finding people worse off to remind us to be grateful and to help.

At this point I want to bring your attention to my style of writing. You might have noticed already, or you will notice as what other books do, I don't tell you to go and do something that I have not tried myself in my own life. As you noticed I am giving you real examples from my own or people close to me because I have lived this book and the only reason, I am writing it, it is because I have seen results from following these steps, so I am sharing it with you. In this book I have been vulnerable with you my reader by telling you I am a human being too and I had to climb the stairs too.

Now as I write the book I revert always to true stories, circumstances, and situations that I have been through and things I have experienced – what I have read, learnt, and listened to – that I have subscribed to and paid for to better myself. I do this because I want you to understand that it is not just about reading my book. I want you to understand there are people who only share a theory of life with you and few dos and don'ts, then they leave you to experience the practical part alone. That is exactly what schools and universities do, then when you are out of the education environment, you realise how the reality of life is different.

I am sharing the practical and real-life examples with you, because I lived every moment of this book. It is to inspire you, because if I can do it, anyone can do it. It only requires you to make a decision, have the determination to achieve the results you want and be willing to ask for help if you need help to move forward.

Still, my book can only help you to lay the tracks. My book can only help you put your train, your mind train, your wealth train on the tracks of Minds2Wealth.

Now, for your soul to be at its happiest, you have to control how your mind feels and how your body feels and by tackling all of the areas of this model, your mind and body can be the best they can be.

During the past few years of personal development, I have continuously asked myself questions. You might recall that I earlier I asked three questions:

Who are You?

What do you want from life?

Why do you want that?

And I am going to keep asking them because 90% of people when you ask these questions do not know what to answer. Right now, I want you to concentrate on what you want from life. Do you know what you want from life? For some, that is quite a hard question to answer.

Money is not necessarily top of the list: money comes and goes. For some, it is being able to see their children develop and grow and to have the time to be with them whilst their business is growing. People might want to be the very best in their field because they love what they do and the people they work with, so it's not actually a job.

Many people when you ask this question, they get stuck, and they do not know what to answer. I was one of them because I was measuring everything with money, because I was desperate to have more money, because I was poor in my pocket and in my head. Now I am considering, "Would it be shallow to just choose money, and wealth or should it be something higher?" and of course it should be something beyond you. We only achieve happiness and success if we are serving others without judgment.

It would have taken me about 2 seconds to answer that before my accident, because it would take me 20 second to assess who is somebody with whom I was dealing? It would only take few questions to decide how I see that person.

The questions in my head were, is he a rich person? Is he going to make me money? Or am I not going to be able to make money out of this person? "If I'm not gonna make money, it's a waste of time to spend time with them." But now I don't even care if somebody has got money and is rich or what status they have. There is no way you can buy me with wealth because I am not a slave to money anymore; it is only your personality and the energy inside your heart that matters to me when I am deciding on how to deal with you, and not your money or status.

I love making money

On the other hand, I love making money, because in my travels to Tibet and my time with monks, I learnt that I could have money and still be a good person. I could be making money and helping more charities to serve humanity. You see, it is not the money itself that makes people be good or bad, it is the intention that they use the money for. My mission is to impact at least a million people in a positive way, and I am sure having money will help my mission and make it easier, even though it is not the main tool I need.

Mother Teresa did not have money but impacted many people with her smile and love. You see I learnt that everyone was born with a gift in them. My gift was to make more money and help charities so they can help people on the ground and that makes me happy.

Some people feel that they should not say money because that is greedy or in some way not valid. You need to change this mindset though. For years I gave time to helping the homeless.

At the time it was all I could give. Now though, I have wealth because my mind is in the right place. Now because I have wealth, I can help many more homeless people than I ever could have done physically.

We all have one body, and the same 24 hours in a day. It is good to give some of that time to helping people. But money gives you the chance to help so many more people. Having money, even vast amounts of money, does not take away your humility. It does not stop you being humble or being kind. It does stop you being needy, so that the people who are helping others have one less person ... or more likely one less family to worry about!

We are talking of helping people and this is one of the ways that we can feed the good wolf as we talked about it in the last chapter.

I will remind you once again to look at these three questions:

Who are You?

What do you want from life?

Why do you want that?

CHAPTER 4

They said I was Crazy to Go on a Personal Development Journey

What is Personal Development? Well according to the Business Dictionary, it is:

"The process of improving oneself through such activities as enhancing employment skills, increasing consciousness and building wealth."

So, why if you say you are doing Personal Development do people treat you like you are an idiot. They seem to think it must be a scam and that you are not seeing the obvious. After all, who wants to be more employable, have increased consciousness, or to build wealth? Well, I did … so I ignored the scoffers and began my journey.

I do not know if it is the money it costs, the time that you have to dedicate to it or the effort and hard work it takes that makes people feel the way they feel until they see the improvement in their life…

People who have not done it by the way, will say that personal development is not worthwhile. For me it was a lot of courses, a lot of money, and a lot of time. Mostly, it was the effort and struggle with my mind that was the hardest. Was it worth it? Absolutely. Would I go through it again? Yes, I do… constantly.

A friend of mine once said a pearl of wisdom that has always stuck with me. It was this: "Personal development is like taking a shower … it is no good doing it once and thinking you are all set, you have to do it every day. "

I have a routine which helps me to include self-development into my life on a daily basis. First thing in the morning after brushing my teeth, emptying my bowels, and washing my face, I go back to my warm bed for meditation and some journaling and setting my day goals. I choose to show gratitude for what I already have first. Gratitude for simple things such as being able to wake up because many people don't wake up in the morning and I used to take that as granted. I show gratitude to the universe by being thankful for every new day and the gifts that I have. I will also show gratitude by wishing people happy birthday and liking ten posts on social media. I will then do several activities. I like to go for a walk around the reservoir locally and immerse myself in nature.

When I get back, I will do yoga. At 1pm I finally have breakfast, and only then will I answer messages unless I know that I have something urgent going on. All these things form part of a routine that keeps my mind and body happy. I also watch inspirational and informative videos and read books to nourish my mind and feed the good wolf.

By 2pm I will be ready to look at forex, stock market and crypto to see if there are any investment opportunity for the day. By 3pm I will look at new business opportunities or do some home education with my children. I avoid the news as it always concentrates on the bad stuff that is happening. All the time good stuff is happening too, people are being born and Spring is coming, but watching the news you would never know.

Bad news sells. And the trouble is that we become filled with negativity. It is important to be positive and to fill our minds with feelings of positivity. Does this mean that I don't know what is going on in the world? No. Did I fail to notice the pandemic? No. Important news will always find its way to you. But we don't need to know every depressing fact about everything. Some of this is now past and we cannot change it, other things are just rehashing the same information from another point of view. Much of it is conjecture and opinion not really news. This kind of negativity has a massive effect on how you feel, what you think and the decisions you make.

Part of my self-development journey involved spending a week with multi-millionaire John Butcher as I have previously mentioned. This was a very important step for me, and during it I created a 178-page life plan. If it is good enough for a multi-millionaire, then why wouldn't it be good enough for me? Or for you? The first goal I set in there was to trim my environment and control what I was watching, reading, and listening to, so I could oversee what would appear in my life. I stopped watching news completely.

My research into successful people lives showed me, almost every self-made millionaire and multi-millionaire will talk about their journey of self- development and how they had to be rich in their mind before they could be rich in their pocket and that is exactly what Tony Robbins told me in one of the sessions I had in his live courses.

New York bestselling author Bob Proctor talks about being broke until he was told to take a copy of Think and Grow Rich by Napoleon Hill and read it every day. He did just that, and if you see him speak you will see his worn and well-thumbed copy of that book which he still reads despite being able to quote whole passages of it. You can download a free copy of Bob's book You Were Born Rich, and it is exactly the kind of book that you should be reading on a constant basis.

http://pardot.s3.amazonaws.com/marketing/You%20Were%20Born%20Rich%20Book.pdf

Also having a coach or mentor is essential in your journey. A coach will keep you accountable and help you stay on track. A coach can help you to achieve your full potential, can empower you, can help you find your why. You might answer why what? That is a great question. And it takes me back to the three main questions:

Who are You?

What do you want from life?

Why do you want that?

These are the questions that you need to keep asking, but to get to where you want to be you need to know "Your WHY."

What do I mean by your "Why"? Your why is a very strong image of what you really want deep down inside. Something that when we think about it causes a feeling in our gut. That is your real why. That is what will drive you to achieve the results you want. If you keep asking the three questions that we have been asking and will continue asking throughout this book you might get there. Some people need a little help.

If you are struggling use the help of a coach who can lead you to the answers you did not know you knew. Later in this book I will tell you more about my Minds2Wealth Programme and our coaching sessions. There will be an opportunity for a few people to work with me in our group coaching sessions or if they need more individual help, then they can take on one to one session with one of our trained and qualified coaches. This is just one of the things I can help you find.

But why does it matter?

Why is YOUR WHY so important? Because it gives you a road map for your journey. In your journey you will face many obstacles and your why, becomes the anchor that you can use to motivate you to continue in your journey.

It is all about how bad you want it.

Do you want it bad enough to do **whatever it takes**? Your true "why", the one that gives you a churning feeling deep in the pit of your stomach when you think about it, and the one that make you feel fired up to get up and do something about an uncomfortable situation you are in. That is your real and deep why, you need to have when starting any success journey, if you want to be successful. We have to feel uncomfortable where we are and have the want feelings for a change and not the need feelings. Only feeling the need for a change is not a strong desire for us to start moving and start the change process. The change process only starts when we step out of our comfort zone and challenge the status quo. Through my journey I learnt we only do whatever it takes when we want to change our situation and it has nothing to do if we need to change it. Our only reason to take action is if we want it so bad and to wanting it so bad, we need a strong reason and strong why to push us to take action.

So right now, I would like you to ask yourself … what is my why?

Coaches can help you unlock the answers you know. Mentors have been there already, and they know what you do not. They know what it is like to hit the wall and keep going. In the journey of success, you need the help of both coaches and mentors. They both know how to keep going, and at Minds2Wealth program we have them both and they can lift you up and help you get back on track.

Coaches and mentors are essential to anyone going through self-development. As a process it can be tough, and we need other people who are on the same page to support us. We cannot turn to friends and family. These are the people who are likely to be saying that we are crazy. We need like-minded people surrounding us.

We need people who know the process to tell us what the next step might be. We need role models. If we have never known anyone who has done self-development, then you need someone who knows what it feels like and who believes it is worth the effort.

You might feel that you are the pioneer for your family and that they will benefit in future because you are better. They don't understand this though. They might benefit from your improved temper, improved income, or improved self-confidence. But they do not know this now.

They might see you struggling and say, "Don't put yourself through this". They might see you spending money on courses and feel that you should have spent it on a new car or a holiday. They might see you spending time watching inspirational talks or reading books and feel that you are wasting time you could be spending with them. Being a lonely pioneer is hard though. It is much easier to get anywhere with company. I understand that deeply because I am the only and the first person in my whole entire family for generations, that has started the self-development journey and also, I am the only and the first person in my whole entire family that has made the amount of money I have made. So, as you can see, more self-development also means more money other than feeing great every day.

So going back to the different areas of self-development I will remind you that they are mental, social, spiritual, emotional, and physical. In the last chapter we talked a lot about the mind, about strengthening it, cutting the weeds, and feeding our good wolf. In this chapter I want to talk about the emotional area.

As you might remember I said earlier that I do not believe that we can control our emotions. But we can learn to respond to them in a more positive way. Angry Ali was the product of me reacting to my emotions with that straight to guns response. My brain said I was being attacked…my emotions of anger and hurt welled up and I responded angrily.

Emotional intelligence is as important as mental intelligence in achieving our goals. It allows us to build good strong relationships with people and we need people along our journey. Family and friends to support us, coaches, and mentors to help and guide us and clients who we support and help. If we are good at building relationships, then we are more likely to find the right people to work with.

If we are angry or lack understanding, then these relationships will be much harder to form. Some people naturally have more emotional intelligence than others, the same as some people are geniuses but we can all learn to respond better to our emotions. The first part of my life was damaged by my lack of understanding of emotional intelligence.

I am very thankful now that I can help other people. When life is difficult it can be tough, not to allow ourselves to be controlled by our emotions. Old Angry Ali would feel emotions and react unchecked, like a child who has a tantrum when they cannot achieve something. Now I am very different, but you see the emotion will still come. I cannot control that feeling that things are not right and that I am frustrated about it. It took time for me to recognise this, and still more time for me to learn how to respond. But I have learned to control my response and reaction which puts me in charge of my emotions.

If you are facing too many problems and feel overwhelmed, then stop. Take seven deep breathes and then look again. There are few situations where there is not time to take seven deep breaths, and these are likely to be situations of feeling anger or overwhelm. If something is happening and there is not time to take breaths, then your emotion will more likely be fear or panic. If it is fear, then you will probably have a reflex response such as if an accident could occur.

Breathwork is a whole subject which is worth knowing more about. In the meantime, practice using the seven breaths.

Another way we can become more emotionally strong is to take on five a day. We have all heard that we should have five portions of fruit and veg a day.

Well, I recommend a further five:

1. Have gratitude.

2. Stop negative things such as news going into your head. As I said earlier what goes in has a massive effect on you.

3. Make sure you have plans for good things to go into your head such as attending seminars and reading books and having successful friends around you to lift your thoughts.

4. Choose who you take advice from and if they have achieved what you want to have. What is the intention of the advice? The intention behind advice is so important…sometimes people, or family members even, give you advice to not to try something and the advice is out of their own fear or jealousy. But if someone has achieved what you want to achieve and they give you advice as your mentor to help you achieve your goals, then it is good to listen, because good advice can be very valuable… and bad advice is very costly.

5. Create an auto block habit. You do not have to read or listen to the end of something to decide if you should read or listen to it.

Sometimes as someone starts talking, you can feel where it is going and intentionally choose to close your ears or walk away. It is ok to walk away from an uncomfortable situation, trust me, I know how hard it is to walk away when you are getting hurt.

You think you have an obligation to stay but you come first… walk away.

I don't blame those who criticized my decision to go through this process though. After all, you don't know what you don't know, and I constantly find more and more things that I don't know as I go through this process. Because of this I constantly move on and update my knowledge. My Rebirth Eye model is the work of many years, but it is unlikely to be the finished article. It will develop as I develop and will be improved so that I can better help you to develop.

During the pandemic, many people have had a lot of anxiety, and many have had a loss of passion and direction. Recent statistics have shown that 7 out of 10 people renting homes in London want to move out. Being able to work from home means that they now see they could have a better work life balance and that they could be living somewhere much more affordable giving them more disposable income.

Still more people have suffered this uncertainty and decided that they no longer feel aligned with what they are doing, or worse, no longer have a job, and they wonder ... what's next? If this is you then personal-development is essential.

If you are saying to yourself ... I want to move on to the next level then maybe my Minds2Wealth programme or the 1:1 coaching we offer might be for you. It might help you to identify your aspirations for the future and to overcome obstacles.

Once again, consider:

Who are you?

What do you want from life?

Why do you want that?

CHAPTER 5

When I Saw the New Man in the Mirror It was Me

What we are talking about now is transformation.

There are so many people that are so afraid to start something because they don't think the time is right, they don't think they have the money, they don't think they have the ability to do it, they don't see the sense in it. It isn't exactly what they want to do and so many other stories in their head stopping them taking a step forward. That is why if you look in my Rebirth Eye model, in the effort to change your story section, I have expressed the importance of a great story to help you make progress. A powerful story to encourage you to win more.

I am proud to say that I have no regrets, most people have regrets, but I do not. If I went back, I would probably do it all again. I have done everything in my power to not be blamed when I am older, to not be questioned by my son, why didn't you do this? Because that it is what I asked my father. I have done everything in my power not to have regrets and when I look in the mirror, I do not see any. I have lost and I have won but there are no regrets.

And that in itself is very powerful and comforting to me. You may be reading this book right now and you may have some form of regret. The best way I can describe regret to you is carrying a bad smell around with you because as I've said before:

Yesterday is history,

tomorrow is a mystery

but today is a gift,

which is why they call it the present.

But let me explain to you how I came to know this and how I learned not to have regrets.

I spend a lot of time in care homes, and I spend a lot of time in cemeteries because I want to show myself this is where I am going to end up. The end for everyone is always death, but the difference between people is that some people live the life until they die but some people are dead from the moment they become adults while they are still alive because they have lots of fear in them. The people with fear never try anything and they always have lots of regrets. NOO, not me! I would rather risk trying something and fail at it, instead of living with regret of not doing it all my life. Life is too short, and I love to experience it fully. So, I should not have a fear of trying. I go to care homes to see people at the end of their life to spend time with them. That is the time when nobody judges you and you have no fear but also you don't have time anymore to try new things. I usually ask them what is your biggest regret? Most say looking back, the only regret they have is why they did not try the things they felt it was right or necessary. Their regret is why did they care about what people say or think… They usually say, I wish I had done what was right in that moment, but I did not because I feared the result.

So, the four biggest regrets people at the end of their life usually talk about is:

1. I wish I would have tried things I never tried because of the fear. I wish I 'd had the courage to live a life true to myself, not the life others expected of me

2. I wish I would have spent more time with my friends and family. I wish I would have stayed in touch, so now I would not be feeling lonely.

3. I wish I would have loved my friends, family, and others more and I wish I would have given the permission to myself to live a happier life by having the courage to express my feelings correctly.

4. I wish I would have created an investment portfolio or some sort of income for myself to not struggle in my old age.

So, from that experience, the only fear I have is the fear of having regret when I am older at the end of my life. So, I paid attention to other people's regret at the end of their life. They are the warning lights life gives you, but most of us ignore the life warnings, so we end up living a regretful life in our older age. The regret cycle gets repeated because we do not learn from other people's life experience. I love learning from other people's experience and knowledge, that is why I always go to courses and get mentors and coaches, because learning from other people's experience has saved me lots of time and money.

As Isaac Newton said it...

'If I have seen further than others, it is by standing upon the shoulders of giants'

-Isaac Newton

You only make more progress than others if you stand on the shoulders of giants who have tried life before you by learning from their experience.

My advice to you is to be afraid of the regret you could feel at the end of your life for the things you did not try. Do not be afraid of judgment by others and where the road is going to take you. Just do it, just take it, and see where it takes you, and remember, you always can come back to where you left at the start of your journey. The difference is, by not taking the journey, you never know if that was your personal journey you were born to take or not. At least you can look back and say, you know I lost, but I have no regret, because at least I tried it.

You also can save a lot of time by taking calculated journeys instead of just any journey in life. I found that, calculated path and journeys takes you where you want to be, but uncalculated and unplanned journeys can make you end up where you do not want to be. Having a role model and learning from other people's life experience can be a very good guide for you in your journey planning and selection methods, because you can see their results. That is why having mentors and coach in the life journey is so important.

The point about chapter five is that if we have had the ability to move forward if we have the courage and conviction to move forward then we will look in the mirror and we will see a different person. We will look and we will see somebody that we can really thank that they had the courage, that you had the courage, that we had the courage to be able to move forward.

Let me ask you this question. How do you want to feel at the end of your life when you look in the mirror? How do you want to feel? Do you want to look back and think, wow look at this master piece I created! Then look at all your critics and say, what you are seeing behind me, is my creation. Then pat yourself on the shoulder and say, I am proud of you, well done, you did it.

Do you want to be proud of what you created, or do you want to look back and say I could have done this, I could have done that, but I did not do any of it? How do you want to feel? You must decide now because it takes time to build that image in the mirror. It won't happen overnight. You must start now to be able to see the results in the future. Just remember, your past 6 years of life results does not have to match the result of the next 6 years of your life. You can change the future result by taking different action now. You should also remember, never is too late, you always can start now to build your future.

You may be reading this book right now and you might be wanting to record your first song. You might be reading right now and want to start up a nanny agency or wanting to share your story the same way that I've done because you believe that you have something to teach through your life's experiences. Whatever it is that you are feeling inside, I can promise you this: that nothing is ever finalised, nothing is ever finished.

There are no final works, there is just an ongoing development, change and transition in terms of you, the way you think, the way you act and ultimately what you do every single day. But there is only one calling, you have to ask yourself this question: What is your calling?

Every single one of us was born to play a part in this jigsaw. The universe is a jigsaw and every single one of us has a part to play. What is your calling, what are you supposed to do? What is that one skill you have that you can do effortlessly with very little, or maybe even without any, training? Can you play a song? Can you fix a tyre? What can you do without any effort, without any extra training, or that you learn so easily that it is a pleasure?

This is your calling. I can speak, I can trade, what can you do? I went to music sessions for five hundred hours and I still cannot play a note. I was not born to be a musician, but I was forcing myself to make my dad proud. What is your calling? All you have to do is find that calling and then you can start making money. If from that calling you can just make one dollar, all you have to do is just expand that calling.

One dollar to ten dollars, ten dollars to a hundred dollars, one hundred dollars to a thousand dollars. That is how you become rich. Are you good at buying houses? Go and buy a house, two houses, three houses and keep expanding. That is all you have to do. Share your gift with people, do what you love and follow your calling, your purpose.

The Bible says:

Therefore, my brothers, be all the more eager to make your calling and election sure, for if you practice these qualities, you will never fall.

2 Peter 1:10

By moving forward, by having the courage and strength to move forward, by accepting that we may not know exactly where we are going but we are going there, we are learning something. We push forward and it is only by pushing forward that we will ever end up in a place where we need to be. But moving forward on our own is hard, maybe impossible.

Every mind has a different tool, every mind has a different gem. If we work together then we can learn from each other.

Nobody ever knows everything…

That is why a few minds coming together, are always more powerful than one mind. They are more powerful especially if, they learn how to work with each other not against each other.

When I passed my GCSE's, I thought I knew everything, I thought I was the god of knowledge but when I went to university and did more and more courses, I realised that there are more skills out there that I know nothing about. It is not possible to learn all of this by yourself.

Now for those of you that are reading this book right now and have not yet realised or not yet discovered what your purpose is, you may need help to cultivate that idea, to extract the skills and the ability and perhaps discover your why. At the end of the book, you will be able to find out more about how I can help you with my Minds2Wealth programme in which our trained coaches spend one to one time with every single person that joins the programme, in order for us to help you to find your own clarity and your own why.

One of the things we do for you in the programme according to the Rebirth Eye Model in the Better Yourself section is to help you find the right role model. Having the right role model helps you to plan your journey and know exactly where you want to go, so you can get there. Your role model should be the person that you want to see in the mirror.

They should be someone who has already achieved what you want to achieve, they should represent the values that you want to represent. Once you have your role model then you have a route map because you can follow in their footsteps.

As Socrates said…

'The more I learn the more I realise, I know nothing'

-Socrates

As you are reading through my book, I will always refer you back to the three questions at the end of every chapter:

Who are You?

What do you want from life?

Why do you want that?

However, this is now the fifth chapter of my book, you are halfway through reading the book and I want you also to understand that the book is something that I have written to help you in terms of the authenticity and accuracy and truth in terms of my own journey.

I shared my story warts and all so that you might be connected through it to your own circumstance and that it might help you. I want you to understand completely that my book in itself, is not enough to help you move forward in the journey.

I want to finish this chapter on something that is vitally important. You may still be reading this book and you may be at the stage which according to Dr Michael Beckwith is the victim mode.

If you have not watched his video yet you can follow this link:

https://www.youtube.com/watch?v=_Qey1CXTnFE

Now you might still be in a slight stage of victim mode, and you should not regret being at that stage because 90% of people live their lives entirely in that stage unless they decide to move forward. Your brain has been designed to keep you safe, not to accept responsibility, to try to find someone or something to blame. If something is wrong, you are afraid to take responsibility. You are designed to blame someone else.

Even in the case of religion have you ever noticed that people always **blame God. Insurance policies can include "acts of God".**

Where do I start to not be a victim anymore?

Being aware of the problem is the first stage of change.

Being aware of the problem can be one of the most painful experiences because sometimes when we are aware of the problem, we may not like what we see, we may not like who we are, we may realise that we could be a better person. The reason that you feel down is that you realise that massive change is needed and every single one of us fears change. So, it is not just you, and you are not alone in your journey.

Do you remember when you were a child and you had to learn to swim? Or when you had to learn to drive? You had to go through the pain of fear, of being scared of drowning or having an accident first, to then be able to start swimming or driving.

Probably you hated the person teaching you how to swim. Do you remember when you learned how to ride a bike? At that moment you probably hated your dad, mum, or the person who taught you how to ride a bike because they put you through that pain. But how did you feel when you started riding the bike? You felt amazing because you felt the success. When you learned how to drive there were probably times when you hated your driving instructor, because they had to put you through the pain of having to learn how to control the car and to be safe. But how did you feel after when you passed your driving test?

So, always remember when you are going through the pain, don't worry. Going through the pain is the path to progress and change so you might experience fear, but the success lives on the other side of the fear. If you ever wanted to achieve any kinds of success, you should overcome the fear of the journey to that success.

Again, let me repeat the title of the chapter, When I Saw the New Man in the Mirror it was Me. I hope that as you move forward, the person that you see in the mirror in the future after you have decided that you want to take action and change, that you too will look back to see just how far you have come and transformed the person that you have become.

I hope you will be able to say, like me: I am proud of you and the person that you have become. I am proud of what you have created, and I have no regrets.

So now we are halfway through the book have your answers to the three questions changed?

Who are You?

What do you want from life?

Why do you want that?

CHAPTER 6

Every Step You Take, Every Move You Make, Makes You Who You Are

In this chapter I am going to take you through the rest of my Rebirth Eye Model.

Before we get there though, as we discussed in the last chapter, your first step to change is to accept that there is a problem and that you need to change.

Congratulations … you have taken the first step because you are reading this book and you would not be unless you believed that there was a change to be made.

The second step is to identify where you are on Dr Michael Beckwith's model. Like myself and 90% of people you are probably starting at the victim stage and can move on to the manifestation stage, from there you can progress to the level of just being and finally the level of godly.

You cannot move on without doing self-development and my Rebirth Eye model can be a guide to you through this journey to show you want you need to do to move to the next stage.

These steps are:

- Raise your standards

- Efforts to change your story

- Better yourself

- Inspire yourself

- Reset your beliefs

- Train yourself to make good decisions

- Hold on 100%

I have mentioned these previously but now I am going to talk about the area that we not spoken about in more depth and then talk about how to go about it. I suggest you like and follow my Minds2Wealth podcast, as every week on Tuesday 8pm, I go live with one of our qualified coaches and we have a discussion about different elements of this model, and it is free.

Simply search @Minds2Wealth or @realalishahraki on any social media to find us.

Also add yourself to my Facebook group of successful people as I always share my podcast in my group. Simply follow this link to add yourself to my Facebook group:

https://www.facebook.com/groups/minds2wealth

Or follow me on LinkedIn by searching @realalishahraki

Raise Your Standard

Raising your standards is about having higher expectations of yourself. Be hungry for change and be willing to put in the effort it will take to achieve it. Examine your motives for things. Why do you want to do something? Is it going to support your purpose?

Being hungry is essential to achieve success. Someone once asked Steve Jobs, "What keeps you motivated?"

Steve Jobs replied – "My hunger for success. My hunger has destroyed my fear of failure. Being hungry is the key element of my success. I am not satisfied with what I achieved yesterday. I want to make progress, to innovate, to grow and to revolutionize the world."

"Be ambitious and passionate about what you are doing, and success will find you"

– Steve Jobs

Look at your environment, is it inspiring? Is it a good environment to work in or is it messy and disorganised?

Clear away rubbish which will hold you back, do you need some shelves or organisation system? Make it an environment you can be inspired and effective in.

Who do you surround yourself with? Are they people who care about you and support you? Are they uplifting people who understand or if not understand at least support your choice to start your journey of self-development?

Are they people who bring you down every time they enter the room? Are they the kind of person that makes you feel down when you are around them? These are people that you need not to have in your life. Raise your mood by spending your time with people who understand what you are doing and are on the same kind of journey themselves.

Raise your mind. Read the right kinds of books, do training and webinars. Learn the things that will support your journey to where you want to go, to be the person you want to be, the person you need to be to fulfil your purpose. You also need to take back control of your thoughts. People have what is known as Automated Negative Thoughts. This is the little voice telling you that you are not good enough, that you didn't do this right or that you are chubby or stupid.

We need to kill these ANTs. Stamp on them. Wipe them out. Give them no room to nest. When they come crawling along stamp on them immediately with positivity. Make sure that there is so much positivity, that the good wolf is so well fed that the ANTs run away to nest elsewhere.

Efforts to Change Your Story

I remember as a child being asked to pass the salt from the cupboard. I didn't want to do it as it meant getting up and walking around the table and I felt grumpy about it. It isn't there I responded to my dad. Yes, I was told it is there and you should go and get it. After resisting and becoming grumpier I gave in with bad grace and went to the cupboard and looked for the salt.

I could not see it. It isn't there I told my Dad …

I told you it wouldn't be.

My father eventually, exasperated, got up and came to the cupboard and there at the very front right in front of my eyes was the salt.

Was I lying to make my father to get up? No, it was the story I had told myself. I told myself that the salt would not be there, so I created a blind spot in my mind. Because of this blind spot I could not see the salt.

This is known as confirmation bias. We tell ourselves stories all the time and some of them serve us, while others don't.

On the other hand in 2014 when I started focusing on making money and accepting the story of I can do it too, instead of saying making money is for rich people, my brain suddenly became so active to find different ways of getting me to money. I started to see opportunities everywhere, it was amazing. I learnt that whatever you want to see in life, that is exactly what you will see and find in front of you. So, I changed all the stories in my head. Instead of looking for sickness and cancer, I look for health, instead of looking for excuses to stay poor I started to look for money. Instead of looking to blame I started to forgive more. Instead of seeing the empty part of the glass I started to see the full part and my life suddenly changed.

Let me share a story with you to help you even more to understand, how you can change your life perspective by changing your story.

A couple are on a journey in a car and the lady asks the man if he will pull over so that she can use the toilet. The man responds no. The lady begins to tell herself the story that her husband doesn't love her anymore, if he loved her, he would surely pull over. Maybe he is having an affair. You see that story will ruin her relationship with that man.

But she could choose to tell herself a different story. Maybe he knows there are no services before the exit they are taking, maybe they are running late and knows that it will not take much longer to get to the destination. She could tell herself that there must be a good explanation and that she can be patient and wait. She can choose to see the half full side of the glass. By doing that she strengthens her relationship and will enjoy more a loving relationship instead of a life of argument.

What stories are you telling yourself that are not serving you? Can you think of a better story to tell yourself instead? You can do this with things that trouble you from your past as well. Is there a better light that an experience can be seen in? How did this experience happen for you to help you to be the person that you are today; the person choosing to become a better version of themselves?

It can be hard to see who you want to be before you have achieved it. Therefore, it is important to find yourself a role model.

Better Yourself

We have covered some of this section earlier. A great mind needs a great body. What is the point in striving to be the best you can be if you do not give your body the same care that you give your mind? You need your body to enjoy the fruits of your success. You might want to achieve all of this so that you can spend time with your family.

In that case you need to be healthy enough to spend time with your family, you need to be fit enough to go on the country walks or skiing trips. You need to be well enough to enjoy those holidays together. What is the point of it all to finally have all of the things on your wish list but to be in a wheelchair and unable to enjoy any of it … or worse?

You need to eat healthily and take regular exercise. I recommend you find someone to work with you.

Someone who can guide you and keep you accountable. I recommend this for all areas of your life in which you would wish to make an improvement and the same goes with your health.

I talked about trimming the weeds. Get your mindset into good order. Sort out those relationship issues and things that have happened in your past that are making your mind garden untidy.

Back to the better yourself module and you will recall that I said you should find yourself a role model to inspire you and, in whose footsteps, you can aim to follow. As I said, I chose Sir Richard Branson. Choose someone who has achieved things you would like to achieve and whose values you believe in. Remember that they have paved the route that you want to take so be prepared to follow.

Inspire Yourself

It is easy to get inspired by someone or something and then go away and the inspiration wears off. Then when things get difficult, life gets in the way and because you are no longer buzzing with that initial wave of excitement that had us hitting the ground running you end up slowing down and you are no longer the rolling stone. You begin to gather moss and if you are not careful you will stop altogether and give up on your dreams ... after all life is fine as it is, right? But is it?

As I mentioned I have visited lots of care homes and talked to the residents. Do you know what they regret? They regret the things they didn't do ... not the mistakes they made along the way. Whenever we try things, we make mistakes, and we can choose to fall forward or become stuck in the mud and not try new things. These people do not regret the falling ... they regret being sticks in the mud.

Aren't your dreams worth pursuing? If not, then I suggest you find new dreams. Ones that are worthy of your efforts.

To stay on track though you need to find new inspiration to help you get past the inevitable roadblocks, naysayers and life's nagging little chores. And seeking to stay inspired is high up the list of things that you need to do daily......Like showering, if you don't you might find that life begins to have a bad smell!

I regularly read books such as the autobiographies of successful people. I like to watch inspirational and motivational speakers, go to events, listen to uplifting music. I start my day with something inspirational and top it up whenever the waters start to muddy.

Reset Your Beliefs

Your beliefs are created by what you have achieved, and high achievers exude a confidence that you notice when they walk into a room. They don't need to say anything, but you will notice that air of being comfortable wherever they are.

You need to take action in order to achieve so these people, the high achievers, are action takers. If you never take the chance to try anything then you will never achieve anything. Sure, in trying you will make mistakes ... but did those high achievers get there without making mistakes? No, they are action takers and actions come with the risk ... the almost inevitability of mistakes.

Some of these mistakes will be big and will create failures. The difference between those high achievers and those less successful is not usually their abilities but the number of times they get up.

People who achieve anything, Olympic medals, huge businesses, world records are not always the most naturally gifted or the most intelligent but the most diligent and the most willing to keep getting up when they fall.

Reset your beliefs. You need to remember how many wonderful things you have achieved and that you have an amazing capacity for achievement. The human brain is full of brain cells that together form a computer that is capable of storing every piece of information in the world. It is faster than a computer and while it is a myth that we only use 10% of its capability it is certainly true that most of us have the capability to do, to learn, to think way beyond what we currently do.

If you don't have any great ambitions and just want a nice car or a boat that is fine. Go make the money and enjoy the fruits of your labour. There is no rule that we have to all be Sir Richard Branson wannabe's ... but there is also no rule saying that you cannot be a high achiever ... that you could not be that person walking into the room exuding confidence.

All I am reminding you is that God or universe gives us all one golden egg which we call life. We get rewarded even more if we use the golden egg properly. Some of us choose to do nothing with it and just give it back untouched at the point of death when they meet their grave. On the other hand, some of us use the golden egg to invest it, grow it and even make more out of it to use the extras to help and impact other people life. At the point of death those people have a good resume and can show how they used their life to impact the world in the good way. Of course, some people choose to use their life golden egg, in a way that they make life miserable for others and that is again their choice and their legacy.

Tony Robbins has a formula for achievement which is:

$$Action + Certainty = Results$$

This is the way to achieve that kind of confidence that is contagious and makes people want to be around us. As we act on our potential, we will get results and the results will give certainty which will give us confidence to take further actions. Not taking action means we would not see any results and that means we will not feel certain in the decision making process and that makes us be doubtful and low confidence. Being of low confidence means, we find it difficult to make good decisions and that means we would not be achieving our full potential, because we are always worried about the result and outcome of our decision and how people judge us.

I remember my mentor always use to say, the difference between the lion and the elephant and why the elephant is not the king of the jungle is the way they see themselves and their confidence. The lion sees himself as the hunter and the elephant as his dinner, but the elephant sees himself as dinner for the lion so he does not even try to use his strength against the lion…but if the elephant changes his perspective, then he can take on the whole pack of lions. You see in this example, everything depends on who we think, how our belief is and how we see the world and others and all of that determines how we react.

You have a choice to delete some un-empowering images from the time you been hurt which dented your confidence and you have the choice to replace them with empowering images to empower yourself. Some of the images are not useful to your future of to your inner peace and one thing NLP does is teach you the skill to be able to create new images to replace the unhelpful ones and recreate memories which will help you to move forward in life and achieve your inner peace.

In our Minds2Wealth programme, we will be going through some of the practices that I have been through. I have done iron bending and wood breaking, helicopter jumping, bungy jumping to be able to overcome fear. We will be doing wood breaking and iron bending in our Minds2Wealth programme as part of restoring your empowering thoughts.

There is one thing that you can be certain of and that is if you take actions then you will sometimes fail. Each time we fail we learn and if what we learn forms the basis for the next attempt then each attempt should bring you nearer to a good result. Thomas Edison is famed for saying:

I have not failed. I've just found 10,000 ways that won't work.

If Edison had been too timid to try, we would not have many comforts we have in our lives, and he would not have become a legend. He would not be remembered for ever by generations after he was gone. There would be no books written about his amazing life and inventions that changed billions of lives around the world.

As well as seeing yourself as capable of achieving the things you dream of and being willing to fail, you also need to be opened to learn from others. Look for the old man who has made mistakes and ask him for advice. He can tell you which way not to go. You can choose to listen to him or not but at least you will know which pitfalls to expect.

Be around people who have failed. It sounds counterintuitive but people who have never failed are either very young and very lucky or have not attempted much. You want to be around the ones who have tried and tried. I am not talking about people who just kept trying the same thing over and over again and are surprised each time it doesn't work. I am talking about the people who have found many ways not to do it.

Do you think of Thomas Edison as a failure? No! He was a success and famously invented the lightbulb. It doesn't matter that he found 10, 000 ways that didn't work only that he found the one that did. Was it worth getting up and dusting himself down every time a potential new bulb didn't work? Of course. Would it be worth it to you to achieve your dreams? If so, reset your beliefs to… yes, I can, then you CAN achieve whatever you want. If not, then put down this book and go and enjoy yourself doing something you love!

Train Yourself to Make Better Decisions

Train yourself to make good decisions and create good habits. Of course, we can only know if a decision is good in hindsight, but we can train ourselves not to make rash decisions. Rash decisions are not thought out or are not based on sound foundations. Don't be afraid of failing because being able to make good decisions comes from having experience and having experience comes from trying and failing and learning from failures. Don't be afraid to serve and help people on your way because serving people maybe even free at the start, gives you lot of practice and experience. Stop the negative training in your head and fill up your head with positive and hopeful thoughts by having faith in a higher being, meditation and reading.

Hold on 100%

Holding on applies in a couple of ways. Firstly, it applies to our relationships. You will recall that I said that we should give 100% in our relationships. When I started giving 100% in my relationship with my wife, she responded by giving 100% back. Does that mean that we have a 100% relationship? No ... better ... it means that our relationship has 200% percent effort going into it.

I am holding onto this relationship 100% and so is my wife. Do you think our relationship is strong? You bet. Was it strong the day we argued, and I stormed off on my motorbike? Not so much. Was it because we didn't love each other as much as we do now? I don't believe so, although I can only of course speak for myself, but I have always loved my wife dearly.

What would giving 100% do for other relationships? Your relationships with your children? Your siblings? Your friends? Your colleagues? Your clients? Would it be good for business? Probably.

We cannot have expectations though. Just because my wife responded by giving 100% in return doesn't mean that everybody will. That is their choice. But even if they don't, the extra effort that you give is surely going to improve things don't you think.

It is important that once you begin you hold on 100%. On your journey it will sometimes be very tough to keep going without inspiration and mentorship, so it is important to keep going back to that inspiration.

This is where you have to go back to your why. I said at the beginning that this book will be filled with questions and here are more: Who are you? Why are you doing this? Why are you starting this journey of self-development? What do you want from life? Why do you want it?

If you don't know the answer to these questions, then perhaps you should go back to that earlier chapter and work out the answers because it is no good knowing how to get where you are going unless you know where you want to go. I say that I wandered aimlessly doing course after course and visiting leader after leader, but I knew my why even if I wasn't clear exactly how. Without knowing your why, you will not finish the journey because it is your why that allows you to dig to the bottom of your resources.

If you are not able to identify your why then it is something we could work with you on in my Minds2Wealth Programme in one 2 one environment with our trained coaches or in our group coaching settings. It is essential you find your deepest why, because every time you get stuck or feel that you cannot go on, you can return to your why for motivation.

You will remember that I said you cannot control your emotions, but you can learn to understand them, and it is important to understand the fact that YOU HAVE A CHOICE on how your respond to any emotion you might feel.

And you have a choice right now to really look at yourself. This book has been written, designed, and created through between ten to fifteen years of intense personal development that has seen me go through the highest of the highs and the lowest of the lows. The lowest of the lows have been some of the worst points of my life but the lowest of the lows can also come from trying and not quite getting to where you want to go, of facing a setback and thinking I am not quite getting there as fast as I would have liked.

And at other times you are so happy, so pleased that you can achieve exactly what you wanted to achieve and perhaps surpass that on any given day giving yourself total contentment. Be aware that how we feel impacts the lives of others around us. We can choose to be strong, or we can choose to be weak. We can choose to be wise, or we can choose to be ignorant. We can choose to be loving, caring, kind and considerate and we can also choose to be cold-hearted, cunningly rude, obnoxious, and depressed. I choose happiness. We choose happiness.

Let go of any bad feeling you have or any hurt from the past from anybody, of the words they said to you because holding onto the words and the behaviours of others towards you in the past can have a very bad effect on your future. They say that words can heal, or words can hurt but I say that you have a choice to let that word heal you or hurt you.

You might have been told you were stupid as a child, but you have a choice to believe that or not. Remember, you are not that child anymore, you are an adult. And if you are reading this and you are a child my best advice to you is to create an antivirus around your head. Press the button when somebody is saying something to you which you feel is hurting you and let the antivirus save your ears, to save your head from hearing those words.

Unfortunately, you don't have control over other people, what they say to you or how they behave towards you, but you have the choice of accepting it and letting it go or not accepting it and just passing on.

Let me remind you of these 3 questions I have been asking from chapter one, and how all of above help you find answers to these questions?

Who are you?

What do you want from life?

Why do you want that?

CHAPTER 7

Smiling Inside I Found My Inner Peace

As we move into chapter seven, we are talking about how we start smiling inside when we find our inner peace. Now reading this chapter there are going to be different types of characters, different types of personalities. Now depending on the type of personality that you are, what you have learned about yourself and how you feel and what you do to try to reach further than your mind has gone before (and you can be in a constant state of flux), this chapter will have different meanings for you.

For people who are not highly spiritual it will mean one thing to you. If you are a very spiritual person, then you will understand exactly what this means. In order for us to find an inner peace it is constant work in order to get ourselves into a state of happiness. Happy where we are in our lives. Happy where we are in our relationships. Happy with our business and careers. And for many of us we understand that an inner peace is only ever really achieved by working out what is most important to us.

Inner peace is when you see self-control as your strength and being calm as mastering your emotions. In that moment you can be in charge of your intelligence instead of leaving your emotions in charge. Achieving this takes a lot of work and it took me fifteen years of learning and self-development and constant work on my inside to finally feel the inner peace within me, but that is the simple explanation.

Let me tell you a little about how I got to the point of feeling inner peace. As I have said I was a very angry person and I realise that the reason that I was angry was because when I was a child my father spent most of his time with his brother, because his brother had mental health issues. So, my father spent a lot of time helping his mother to care for my uncle who would become crazy and kick off.

As a child I would become jealous. Why was he spending all of his time with his brother and with my grandma, but he doesn't spend that much time with us? Then when he was at home, he would become angry because I didn't understand him, and what he was going through. He had just been through a fight with his brother, but I didn't know this. I started to create hate because I thought that when he was home, he should be spending time with us.

And then he started going on lots of holidays alone to reduce his stress level of dealing with his schizophrenic brother. Now I understand that he was going on holiday to be able to keep going, so he didn't go crazy and to help him to continue being a father and brother. He was basically removing himself from the stress environment to be able to come back to it with a better and calmer mind. As a child I didn't understand why he was going on holiday and leaving my mother and I behind.

Why did he shout at my mum, why is he angry at my mum? I couldn't understand why he was doing this so that created that hate and anger inside of me against my dad. Every time I judged him based on these things, I could never truly feel love inside of me towards him until I was writing my life book in 2016 and he finally said he was very proud of me. Then I could finally let go.

We went to Wales, and we had a massive fight in front of everybody over a bottle of water and it was crazy. I felt ashamed of myself shouting at my dad. It was like two lions trying to claim the throne and say who is the boss. And I let go. The moment I could let go of my anger and my hate towards my dad and his past and what he has done, by understanding why he was doing all this I suddenly felt inner peace. I suddenly felt inner peace within myself. I suddenly felt I can let go now and I can carry on. Finally, I could breathe, and my shoulders felt lighter. I felt, by letting go of the past I could move to the future. I was finally at peace within me.

For ten years I had been arguing with my dad, fighting with my dad, we literally couldn't sit next to each other for ten minutes. If my dad and I were left together for just a few minutes we would get into a fight over literally anything, we could never agree about anything. Fish and chips had to end quickly because we couldn't spend a whole evening together. I tried to avoid spending time with him because we would end up in a fight.

We opened a business in 2017 and after 6 months it was doing well but we couldn't get on because every time I passed by him, he was nagging. I don't like moaners. When I was doing my coaching course, I learned about the Gibbs Reflective Log. I started to write logs for every event of meeting my dad and I would make a plan. I am going to meet my dad for lunch but if he says this trigger word, I am going to give him a hug.

Now it has got to the point where when I see my dad and he is angry, I just give him a hug. I give him a kiss automatically and he just calms down. We don't argue about anything anymore. I started to understand his past and his frustration and how much expectation was placed on him as a young child to look after his brother. My dad was never able to let go of this frustration and anger and passed it onto me.

I spent years hanging onto this anger but finally realised what was happening. I was the man who was able to break the mould because otherwise I could have passed it on to my children. Thankfully because of my journey I was finally able to let it go, to forgive my father and myself and to achieve inner peace.

It's one of the greatest gifts you can give yourself, to forgive. Forgive everybody.

Maya Angelou

The amount of time and energy and cost of love, of money, of wasted time when I wasn't in a place of inner peace I cannot get back. And as I am talking to you now, my reader, my new friend, my new fan and perhaps somebody who will be taking my Minds2Wealth course, I want you to look at your life right now and I want you to look at the things in your life that you feel are holding you back because of the way that your emotions are situated. I want you to look at how your emotions are placed and how you deal with them.

For example, are you somebody that when you are driving along and you accidentally cut somebody up, or you are driving too slow, and somebody drives past beeping their horn and sticking their fingers up at you, are you the kind of person that argues back and screams back? We have all done it. But something I do regularly, now the first thing I do when somebody beeps me or cuts across me, the first thing I do is smile at them, put my hand out of the window and say sorry pal, sorry about that and even if they have carved me up, I say no problem, mate, no problem.

The reason I do that is because I have let go instantly of any potential angst, any anger, any frustration. Meanwhile the other driver that is still hooting will still be frustrated seven, eight, nine, ten miles down the road.

So, we have to learn to let go of many of the challenges that we face. And how did I learn to let go so fast? When I had my bike accident, I realised that I might not be alive for the next hour, so now I live as if this is my last hour. If you had only one hour to live, would you want to spend it being angry at somebody. I wouldn't. I would want to spend it making good memories for the people that I love and live happily. For that reason, I have a timer on my phone, and I give myself thirty seconds to get angry, to get the frustration out. Sometimes I even type a post or an e-mail to the person I am angry with and then I delete it. I don't send it, to simply get the anger out of me so then I can forgive and move on.

Abraham Lincoln and Winston Churchill, two great leaders, used to use this method. Abraham Lincoln wrote an angry letter to his commanding officer complaining that he hadn't listened to him, and that the enemy came back. He didn't send it. Instead, he wrote another letter praising the commander in chief and sent that instead.

Ali Shahraki's golden rule of letting go:

Give yourself 30 seconds to exhale it out, don't keep it in, let if out. Otherwise, you will become like a pressure cooker, and you will blow up.

In the process of letting go you will lose many things from the past, but you will find yourself.

Deepak Chopra

Remember: When you let go of something, you are creating space. The space for something better than what you had in the past…

That could be a past bad relationship, habit, or bad attitude. As soon as you let go, now you are ready to accept a good new habit, attitude or even a better relationship. So let go and be free.

Inner peace is something that needs constant tending, and our mind garden needs constant weeding to stay in that inner peace state, and if we stop working on our mind that lawn will start to grow weeds again and make us lose our inner peace. Achieving inner peace means we will have left behind the victim mode, and we might even have surpassed the manifestation mode and transcended to the being mode or perhaps even have reached the godly, the as me mode.

This is a short video in which Dr Michael Beckwith explains these levels of spiritual awakening if you haven't watched yet I highly recommend you watch it.

https://www.youtube.com/watch?v=vg-D2DMFbhk

I have been on a journey of forty years of growth and development throughout my life, and specifically the last ten years of my journey has been about very deep search for knowledge and understanding, so that you don't have to take as long as I did. I have made many mistakes on the journey, but now I know where not to invest my time and development, because it didn't make sense, but at the time, I thought it made sense.

I have created all of the scenarios, all of the learning and all of my understanding and I put it into what I call the Rebirth Eye Model.

And if you follow the Rebirth Eye model and can understand it and can accept and embrace it then you have become stronger together. Some of you as always, my dear loved readers, friends, acquaintances, loyal fans and people I have not yet had the humble pleasure to meet, you may still be at a place where you are not really realising what it is you might have to let go of.

And that's okay. Don't be alarmed, don't be afraid and don't be too hard on yourself. Just keep reading the book, because I have always said in every single chapter through this book the three questions which are:

Who am I?

What do I want from life?

Why do I want it?

CHAPTER 8

I Wanted to Give Up So Many Times, But I Didn't

When we have an idea to look at doing something new, a new adventure, a new journey, a new business, a new career change all of us will have a first thought when we become aware … oh my gosh, I want to do this, I am attracted to this, I feel excited by thinking about this.

Then it is a case of, well, should I pursue it and some people in a career have always dreamed of moving forward and have sat there for ten years and never asked their boss for a promotion, never put themselves forward, never had a meeting with their boss to say I think I could be your manager. It is the same thing for people in business when you first have a dream, an aspiration, an idea where lightning strikes your mind, where you are compelled to act on something.

There are a couple of things that happen, you either act upon it, act upon your imagination, follow that vision through or again you sit on it and carry on with your career or carry on with the job or the business that you are doing, and you never actually act on it. Some people may never act on it ever at all and as they say some of the best business ideas have died in the dream graveyard.

But for the ones that do act they then go through a process. To start you have a vision and you start to take action on that vision, and it starts to be very real. If you are moving forward into that real stage where you start to be building it then what is going to happen is this.

You are going to go through such an emotional change, challenge shift and a new dimension of thinking. It is so severe what you go through, what your mind goes through, that you face the things you are learning, and you continue to keep pushing forward and your mindset is so tuned so that no matter what you face, no matter what obstacles you come up against, you will just keep going and you will push it through.

Whether it is something that you are coming up against in your mind, whether you are struggling to believe in yourself, whether you can't yet see it yet, whether you have started to panic because you have got to see this through, and the reality has hit home Holy S**t this isn't as easy as I thought. A lot of people will reach a point where they have started to try and what will happen is that they will turn back.

They will turn back because they will get themselves into a place where they will either want to go back into their warm comfort zone where everything is familiar, or they will proceed and continue into the unfamiliar. And it is this balance between familiar, going back to what we know, the comfort of what we know, the peace and tranquillity of our comfort zone, to being in the unfamiliar and outside our comfort zone where actually the most incredible growth happens.

Now, for us to be successful, and as I say in the title of this chapter, it is about how I wanted to give up so many times, but I didn't. On your journey and as you are reading this book you will want to turn back. Let me take you back to the Rebirth Eye Model where it says hold on 100%, it says give it all you've got. This is because it is your idea, if you don't give it 100% who is going to give it? If you have the expectation that somebody else is going to give 50% and you are going to give 50%, what happens if they don't give 50%? Therefore, it is you and you only that is responsible 100%. Now some of us when we are trying to give 100%, we look at ourselves and we are scared, we feel the fear inside ourselves.

The reason we have the fear inside of us is that we don't know what is going to happen. Every human being has a fear of the unknown because we fear being judged, we are scared of what is going to happen, fear of loss. Am I going to lose, am I going to win, what will people think? The only way to win is to go through the fear and accept the fact you won't know until you go through it. Stop making unreal assumptions about the outcome and just decide based on what you see, and always think what if it does work out? Remember you always can go back to where you started, but you won't know what was waiting for you after your fear.

Let me tell you the story of probability. It was told to me by one of my mentors. He told me, he tried for four years to get to the end of this probability story but there is always two possibilities and cycles keep getting repeated.

The story goes like this… I looked under my bed, and I found a little monster, now there are only two possibilities, either he is going to eat me, or he is going to be my best friend.

Each situation has two possibilities again, so we choose the possibility of, if he decides to be my best friend then there are two possibilities again. Me and monster, either would go to school together or I could leave him at home.

Again, in any of those situations there are two possibilities. So let us forget about the leaving at home option, because that on its own has two possibilities. Either the monster would eat my mom, or they could become best friends, which again each situation would have two possibilities each. So, let's say, if I took him to school with me. The monster either would be a great friend and play with me and my friends, or it might eat all of the children in the school. Again, each situation has two possibilities. And the possibility of each situation is always 50:50. So let's say if the monster eats all the children and the head teacher calls the police which could be one of the possibilities, the head teacher also be eaten by the monster instead of calling the police. Let's say if the head teacher calls the police situation is true, there are two possibilities again. The monster could get caught by the police or it could run away to a nearby jungle. Each of the situation is 50:50 chance again. This could carry on until the monster runs to the forest, finds himself a wife and has children and perhaps his children can be under the bed of your children or maybe not, again all those situations each could be 50/50 chance of being true. This keep repeating as a cycle. The cycle of probability is never going to finish. The probability is always 50:50. So the outcome of anything could be 50% good for us and could be 50% chance of everything go wrong. So, what it is that forces us to focus on the negative part of the equation?

What if you try and this is the best thing that you have ever tried? What if the thing that you have a fear of it is actually the thing that is going to get you to where you want to be? Success is always after the wall of fear. If you have a fear of something just have a go at it, you can always go back to where you are now.

But what if this was the best thing? Just have a go at it. Now, you might have an internal fight when you are trying to make that choice, shall I go through it or not? And the reason that you have this internal fight other than having this fear is because you don't have a strong vision, you don't have a strong why yet. Have you asked yourself today "Who are you, why are you doing this?"

This is a question that we have been going through since the beginning of this book, asking if you know who you are and why you are doing this. Just remember we all have a choice.

Your success depends on how quickly you get up and continue after you have failed. Many people when they get hit don't get up anymore, they stay down, and while they are down, they keep getting kicked. Let me tell you the story of the millipede.

The millipede was a very successful dancer and he had lots of fans. Everyone was coming, watching his show, clapping. There was a cockroach who hated this millipede, he would hide behind the trees watching the millipede, getting jealous, and wondering why the millipede was getting all of the attention. He didn't know what to do but he wanted to ruin the business of the millipede.

So, one day the cockroach went home, and he started thinking and he decided to write a letter to the millipede. The millipede was a very nice person and he used to respond to every letter. So, the cockroach wrote a letter saying "I am your biggest fan. I always come to see your shows. I always clap for you. But I always wonder which is the foot that you put first? Is it foot number 26 or foot number 24?

The millipede started thinking, I am an entrepreneur, I am a dancer, I just do it naturally, I don't think about which foot is going first, but I must answer this letter, I cannot ignore it, he is one of my fans, so I have to answer it. He decides that next time he is dancing that he is going to pay attention and he is going to work out which foot he is putting first.

So that is what the millipede did. He tried his best to work out which foot he was putting first. And what do you think happened? He tripped and fell, he collapsed. He tried again and he kept falling. Nobody was clapping anymore, and the cockroach was watching again from behind the tree the same as usual. The millipede fell again, and everybody laughed. With one letter asking the wrong question the millipede lost all of his fans and all of his business. He went back to his house, locked the doors and he became depressed forever.

The millipede had a choice to come back stronger or to stay locked away. It is the choices we make. Have you fallen yet or are you afraid of falling? Have you tried it yet? If you haven't then why don't you give it a go today? Because trust me I have failed, I have started many businesses and every time I came out okay. I just learned more and more which helped me in my journey. It made me stronger. It made me more resilient.

Let me go back to the cockroach for a minute. Do you have a cockroach in your life? There are some people in life who are negative people, naysayers and they can damage your dream. They are dream stealers, dream killers. What people do you have around you? Are they supportive? Or are there some people in your life who just want to bring you down? Because the people you have around you, the team you have around you determines who you are and what you are going to achieve. Because whenever you feel down the people who are around you could help you get back up. That is why you have to be aware of the people you have around you. On the Rebirth Eye model this comes under Your Environment.

Your environment has a huge impact on you. What is your environment? Who is around you? Where do you live? Which pub do you drink in? Who are the people visiting the pub you drink in? Because if you are drinking in a pub where the president drinks then you are going to meet the president but if you are drinking in the pub where the junkies hang out then you will meet junkies. And trust me the junkies will not get you to be the president, but the president could inspire you to go for presidency. Be aware of your environment, be aware of the people around you but also be aware of the thoughts you are telling yourself.

Again, this brings us back to the Rebirth Eye Model. Be aware of what you are saying to yourself. Are you telling yourself that you cannot do it or can't succeed? What if you try what I tried? What if you tried my jacket if yours is not fitting? I tried every morning for six months getting up in the morning and looking in the mirror and hating myself. I looked in the mirror and I thought I was a fat and ugly person, but I looked in the mirror and told myself, you are inspiring, you are beautiful, you are strong, and it worked. Before that, before I would laugh at all of the motivational speakers thinking what you are talking about?

I was thinking that they were fake, but I realised after 6 months that I felt amazing. What do you get out of self-sabotaging and telling yourself that you can't do it, you can't achieve it? Don't you feel miserable, don't you feel depressed? How about if you try my way and put it in your routine? That is why I said in the Rebirth Eye Model that you have to have a special routine. This should be part of your routine, to look in the mirror and tell yourself "I am amazing, I can do it".

Warren Buffet always says "I have a range of positive vocabulary. When somebody asks me how am I? I always say fantastic, even if I have pain hidden underneath, or I say I am going to be amazing. I never say oh! I am not well, or it is something wrong with me. By admitting you are not well, automatically your brain losses half of the battle straight away. How do you think I defeated Covid three times and Omicron once? I first won the battle in my head by believing the fact I am going to defeat this illness. I refused the whole time to admit I was sick even though I had a 41-degree Celsius temperature for twenty-five days the whole time. I kept telling myself, you are not allowed to give up because you have 4 kids, and they are watching you fight. If I would have given up, I was setting a bad example for my kids. Now every single one has learnt by being strong mentally you can defeat anything. Every time you want to give up under pressure, remember this is life and we all go under pressure sometimes, but remember who is watching you fight. Be aware of your kids, your little brother, sister, or friends who is watching you fight, and you are their only hope. They are all watching you quietly. At least to give them hope, keep fighting to win, but don't struggle. Always ask for help if you feel like you are struggling, maybe you just need a hug, a cup of tea or some coaching sessions from an experienced coach or sometimes a nice chocolate cake brings our mood back. You know yourself better but don't struggle. Just remember, at the end everything will be ok, it is just the journey of going through life sometimes has some stress. Only be worried about what is in your control and not something that you have no control over.

So,

How, do you answer when somebody asks you, how are you? Are you manifesting it for yourself? I am depressed. Well let me tell you, if you are answering that question with, I am depressed or I am sad then what do you think your mind is going to do?

Remember your mind is an imaginary part of your body, literally it will search all of the images in your brain, and it will show you the most depressing images from your life to make sure that you are depressed. How can you get rid of that? By controlling what goes in your head. What are you reading? What are you watching? Who are you talking to? When was the last time you read an inspiring book? When was the last time you listened to a motivational speaker? When was the last time you did a meditation? Again, it goes back to the Rebirth Eye model in which we say Inspire Yourself.

Another thing I want you to understand Mr and Mrs Reader is that you are reading this book for a reason or a number of reasons and that is why we are putting up the same three questions at the start and at the end of every single chapter to remind you and those three questions are: Who are you? What do you want from life? And why do you want it? But it is also important to ask how you are going to get it because taking action is very important, so I also ask you now "what is your plan"? Let us help you as we have specific coaching programmes at our Minds2wealth program to fit everyone's needs and budget.

Remember, there is a difference between not trying because of the fear and trying but failing. Here is the thing, for those who don't try, and for those who at least try. You have already succeeded because you tried, because you pushed yourself to the edge of your learning and beyond it. You pushed yourself to the edge of your beliefs and you have gone beyond it. You have pushed yourself to the edge of a new place and now you will make adjustments after a small failure, and you will push through, but at least you tried.

Let me remind you to revisit the three questions:

Who are you?

Where do you want to go?

Why do you want to go there?

Have you found the answer yet?

What is your plan from now on?

What are you going to do to achieve your dream?

If you are still stuck at the fork in your life and feel confused and lost, I must tell you that you are not alone.

I see many people feeling lost every day. We all do at some points in our life!

You have two choices or continue and be lost or come to Minds2Wealth and let us help you to find your path, clarity, purpose, and your why to get you on the right path. I have done it for myself, I can do it for you too.

CHAPTER 9

Health and Wealth It Comes in that Order

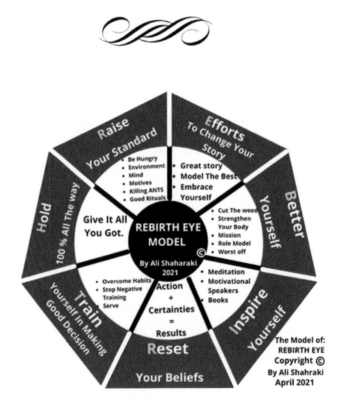

Let me refer you back to the Rebirth Eye model and the section that says better yourself. It talks about strengthening your body.

This is because a healthy mind lives in a healthy body. I talked about this a little earlier but now I will elaborate.

If we are not careful when we are working very hard on our minds, we can neglect other areas of ourselves. As I said, I sat in my chair and learned all about my mind but didn't work on my body ... I hated my body and felt that I was fat and ugly. I dealt with my feelings about my body by speaking to myself every day in the mirror and I still do this exercise every day. It is part of my routine. But what is also part of my daily routine is to care for my body.

You cannot neglect your body because your brain lives inside your body and if your body is unhealthy your brain is not going to survive that long.

You spend a lot of time trying to make money, but why do you want the money? You want to use it to do things you enjoy. How are you going to enjoy your life if your health is bad? What if you cannot eat good foods, if you cannot travel, you can't walk, you can't dance? How are you going to enjoy the money?

Remember why you are making the money. The money is a tool to make your life happy. And what makes you happy is not actually the money, it is the things you can do with the money. But if your health is in danger and you have to be wheelchair-bound and you cannot move around then you may not be able to enjoy it the way you hoped or planned it.

I was at a seminar with Tony Robbins, and they brought a massive wheelchair behind me and reserved three seats for a man. I looked back and felt sorry for this guy thinking I wish he had good health, and somebody said to me that he is one of the world's biggest steel tycoons. He has more money than most people could imagine but he couldn't talk, he couldn't walk, he couldn't do anything. What is the point of having all of that money and not being able to enjoy it? He focused on having money and forgot about himself and forgot about his health.

I know that we want to leave something for our children. But if you ask people who have lost loved ones most will say they would give anything to have one more day with that person. If they would pay a million pounds for just one more day with you then wouldn't it be better to spend that extra day with them, that extra year with them even if looking after your health meant you left them a little less money at the end of the day?

This is why I went to John Butcher to try to find balance, because it can be very hard to find balance, trying to pay attention to everything. Many coaches talk about the different areas of life which we can concentrate on to create life balance. Some people talk about seven areas while others talk about 12. This made sense to me and meant that I was able to pay attention to all of the areas but to pay specific attention to one area for a complete month every year. The categories I use are:

1. Health

2. Finances

3. Children

4. Relationship

5. Intellectual Life

6. Social network

7. Emotional Intelligence

8. Character

9. Spiritual Value

10. Career

11. Quality of Life

12. Life Vision

What I do is to pay attention to all of the areas but focus on one specific area each month. I make sure I create all the habits I need for that specific category in that specific month. Also, I try to update myself on the latest knowledge to improve that specific area of my life before I move to the next category the next month.

I continue in this way through the year and keep moving between categories and keep improving the different areas separately each month. I use the Gibbs Reflective Cycle that I discussed earlier to assess each area and think about how I can improve it. As I mentioned before it takes time to create a new habit, so I don't always succeed in creating the new habits I was trying to form. But it means that every year I have more good habits and less bad ones. Also, some things I try are not as successful as others. That is why this must be an ongoing process.

As we have moved through the various chapters of this book every chapter refers to a different teaching. Every chapter refers to something that I have experienced personally. More importantly as you read the chapter, and this chapter specifically, you will understand that there is a far greater importance in this chapter than perhaps in any other chapter that has been written. Now of course the Rebirth Eye model is made up of seven training modules:

- Raise your Standard

- Efforts to Change Your Story

- Better Yourself

- Inspire Yourself

- Reset Your Beliefs

- Train Yourself in Making Good Decisions

- Hold Yourself 100% All the Way

Each of these modules are designed with the intention to help you to transform, to manifest, to grow and be able to handle, accept and embrace the next stage of your life whatever that may be for you. Whether it is relationships, business or career. Ultimately each chapter is designed to give you a piece of knowledge. In this particular chapter we are talking about health.

And health is something that we can all be lazy with because of lifestyles and the time that we have, or we don't have. Families, running around organising their lives, working extended hours, grabbing food on the go, but your health is vitally important. Why? Because any journey that we undertake in terms of business and business growth, it will cause a strain on your mind and your body.

Now in order for us to be able to achieve the levels of mind strength required to increase our wealth, our happiness and contentment we need a strong body. It is indeed our body, the vessel, the vehicle that needs to be well oiled, well-greased, finely tuned. If you take two different cars on the road as an example:

There is one car that is very fuel efficient, it is very economic, it requires very little servicing because it is well-maintained, and it is kept in the best condition and it is low emission, so it has less impact on the environment. Whereas another car that chugs along hasn't had its oil changed, has not had a service, has not had an MOT, that's not been washed, that's not been cared for or cleaned inside or out and looks like a smoking rust bucket.

The same can be said about the human body. Indeed, what we feed ourselves in terms of our mind and what we feed ourselves in terms of our food determines the levels of energy that we have as an individual. Now some of you will already eat healthily, and you are exercising.

Others reading this book will be more like I used to be. It is very important that we look at this now in this chapter because my role as your coach and trainer and guide during this book is to help you achieve the most amazing levels of mind ability, coupled with asset wealth growth and increasing your profitability. Increasing your money, increasing your net assets in your life. And the most important asset in your life is you, your body and your mind.

Persistence, repetition, persistence, repetition, and consistency….it is no good that you almost half try. This book has not been created for people that want to half try. If you half try, you will fail, and we don't want you to fail at our Minds2Wealth training programme. Therefore, there is the section on the Rebirth Eye Model about giving 100%.

Some of you move forward into the training programme, which you can find out more about at the end of this book and see if you would like to engage with me directly and our group, but for now I am going to make some suggestions for you.

You should know, nobody can say they know everything. In my journey I've understood, it's not about what you know in success, but it is all about who you know and what your team knows to help lift you up. I have surrounded myself with different people who are specialists in their field, and they are good caring mentors and coaches from all around the world.

Earlier in my learnings I realised I could only become an expert in one thing because it is always so much to learn and not much time.

So, I do not specialise in sport, health, and fitness but I specialise in coaching and unlocking people's mind.

So, when it comes to specialist areas, I bring people into my training courses that contribute to my course for you to have the best expert advice that you can. Somebody that is living and breathing that particular field of expertise. For example, if I was to bring somebody in on SEO and marketing, I would bring somebody in who I know has been successful, and my son has been working very effectively in SEO and internet marketing for some time.

If I wanted to bring somebody in who is an expert in business strategy, I would choose somebody who specialises in that area.

If I wanted to bring in somebody who is a specialist in health, I would fetch in somebody who specialises in yoga, in healthy eating and in meditation.

Myself Ali Shahraki, I am an expert in the Rebirth Eye Model, and in transformation and I am here for you to be able to transform your mind and your wealth in terms of the way that you think, and you act, speak and do and I will take you through that journey. But please realise that you will need other experts within your life that will help you.

Now let's talk a bit about health and fitness and why it is so important and what you should consider. Everybody has different values; everybody has a different gift, and everybody has a different level of enjoyment with different sports and fitness regimes. Now I could name lots of different sports and fitness areas for you, it could be cycling, running, or weightlifting, it could be yoga, sailing or football or maybe swimming, tennis or even hiking or trekking. In fact, there are so many possibilities for you to exercise and enjoy exercise.

Thanks to writing this book, now I have managed to create good healthy habits since started writing this book. 1 am focusing on my health. I am tired of neglecting my health and my kids start to notice it and I realised I am setting bad example. So, now my health has become my priority because now it involves my kids, and I will do anything for my kids. You see now I have a very strong why to focus on my health and that is how breakthroughs happens. It is a moment of realisation that your brain accepts your reasons to do something because finally it can see through it. For me I like to get up in the morning and go for a brisk walk around the reservoir to connect with nature and then come back and do some yoga to keep up with my flexibility. But I also love dancing and when I am on holiday you will find me on the dance floor for hours on end and when I come back, I have usually lost about 20kgs! And as I am saying this and talking about dancing it has put a smile on my face because it is something that I really, really enjoy and as I am writing the book I am laughing and chuckling because it brings me joy.

Whatever you choose as your health option, whatever sport you choose, make sure you enjoy the journey, or you will give up halfway.

Rebirth Eye Model is interconnected

You will only start to see positive changes when you embrace all of the seven modules of my training. You must understand the seven parts are interconnected closely and they only work if they are used together.

Let me give you an example, that you go to gym on the first day then you look in the mirror you see no change, then second day, then third day and fourth day but still you see no change. That is the point you want to give up but what does the other 7 parts of the model tells you to do to achieve success in your goal? Give it 100%, tell yourself better stories and so on to be able to continue in your journey. So, as you see this component of the model are interconnected closely and they complement each other. If you follow the model and believe in it, then it will work for you too. It has worked for me for the last 10 years and I can see the results. It has also worked for thousands of others since I put the model out in 2019 in other languages other than English to test it out and now you have the complete version here. I can now class myself as an expert because of the ten to fifteen years of studying that I've pushed myself to do.

I have a degree in Business Management, and an MBA in Business Management but it was after I finished my degree that

I started my real learning. During my degree I only read four books but to get to where I am now, I had to read another 125 books in the subjects of self-development and wealth. I have level 4, in coaching and am ICF registered for life coaching and high-performance coaching, I did level 5 and 6 with Tony Robbins-Madanes in coaching and human behaviour which took three years, and it is the equivalent of another degree.

Then of course I have the experience of all of the businesses that I have run. I started a food shop to test my knowledge in business and it was running really well. I managed to move it from earning £600 per week to £6000 per week by the time I sold it. This is when I went away to work on my mentality. I needed to work on making better decisions and this is one of the areas on my Rebirth Eye Model.

I have taken a journey around the world to see many mentors. After my accident I decided to devote my life to people for free and it was my trip to Tibet which changed my mindset about money. The monk I spoke to was called Ninyo and he said that he understood that I wanted to help people. He asked, why don't you go out and make more money to make a difference to people's lives by helping charities and support us when we are on the ground working.

He told me that I could use the money as a tool to buy food and clothing for homeless people. Some people like to give their time, but you can be more efficient by giving money, you can help more people. This is why I went to learn to make money. I went to see spiritual leaders and hypnotherapists to find out about what happened to me in that accident. I went to Dr Bandler to learn self-control, change my mind, delete bad memories, and create good memories for myself. I did all of that to have a better and stronger mental health.

I went to John Butcher to find how to create balance in life and to Greg Secker to learn how to do trading. I did a two-year mentorship with Aran Curry to learn how to buy and sell properties and to build a portfolio of properties and to choose which strategy to use.

I hired Jim Quick to help me to get my mind straight and from him I learned to Kill the ANTS and to cut the weeds, which you will remember from my Rebirth Eye Model. I learned to be more positive. I have worked with a life coach for the last ten years to help me to get rid of my bad habits. This is not cheap, but I realise that every successful person has someone to talk to. I also read at least one book every single week.

I have studied 50 of the worlds happiest and most successful people, learning about the lives of people like Lord Sugar, Bill Gates, Sir Richard Branson learning how they did it, what habits they had. I also interviewed some of the successful people who I knew, people who earned over a million pounds a year and I asked them how they did it. One of them started from zero and he said it was his education that enabled him to do this. I asked how and he said mindset: you have to fix your mindset, and because of that I focused on my mind, and I focused on my psychology before I started creating the wealth.

In all of this that I have been learning, all of this development, all of this training and realignment of the way that my mind thinks there is one thing that comes of all of this that is specific for this chapter. And we have spoken in the beginning of the chapter about having a health and exercise routine which is physical health. Now I want to come towards the back end of this chapter, and I want to talk to you about something that is vitally important and that is healthy thinking.

You must remember that your feelings are there to help and protect you, but you have to be able to understand your feelings and accept your feelings in any given moment to be able to control your feelings and be able to be in charge. By ignoring your feeling, you just create a volcano which will erupt at one point, and it will cause a lot of damage internally to your mental health. If you don't accept and control your feelings, well then, they will take control and you will suffer by letting your feelings take charge of your life. Every decision you make in your life will be an emotional decisions and emotional decision makers are not good decision makers.

I want to share with you all of the training, all of the studying, all of the development. I want you to experience the growth I have experienced but I cannot do it all in this book. I cannot put fifteen years of education and development, the lessons I learned from the 125 books I have read, all into the book, so I hope that I have given you an insight and a starting point for you to realise that actually I could be the guy to help you move forwards and I look forward to working with you more intensely, with more passion and purpose with some of you that move forward into my Minds2Wealth programme.

And finally, before moving onto the last chapter answer:

Who are you?

Where do you want to go?

Why do you want to go there?

CHAPTER 10

Minds2Wealth is Born

It took me many, many years to research and to study as you know from reading this book, but ladies and gentlemen, here we are this is chapter 10. We are talking about inspiration, we are talking about motivation, we are talking about you, and your gift inside. We are talking about stripping away all of the fear, all of the doubts, all of the resistance that you might have that says that you cannot do something, that you haven't got the skill or the knowledge or the attitude. Ladies and gents, I am here to tell you that you have. When you take away any rejection, when you take away any restrictions, when you take away any fear or doubt all that leaves is the fact that you can do it.

So many people will get trapped inside the fear bubble, the bubble of procrastination that they won't start the journey. So many people will continually talk to you and say, "I can't do this,

I don't understand it, I'm a bit fearful". Ladies and gentlemen, those people are going to be stuck there for ever. If you find yourself saying to yourself, I can't do it, I don't understand it, I'm not going to grow, guess what, you are already training your brain for doom and for failure and you are never going to move forward.

If, however you, like me, are training yourself to say I can do it, I will do it, I will overcome, I will learn as I grow, I will understand that not everything is going to be perfect, if I start today there will become a perfect scenario and situation by default of the fact that I am trying.

On this route of trying when you are pushing forward, when you are creating a new product or a service for your business, or you are trying to move your career forward, you are trying to improve your relationship, the accountability starts with one person … **you.**

You are accountable to you, and it doesn't matter how many books you read. It doesn't matter which lessons of life you take on board, what you have been through, the challenges of life, unless you are prepared to say to yourself, "I can do it, I will do it, I am doing it", you won't. I want you to repeat to yourself, I can do it, I will do it, I am doing it, every single day.

Reaffirm to yourself the motivation that you need to keep moving forward. Let me refer to some very powerful, important businesspeople that you all know right now: James Dyson, Innocent Smoothie drinks, Sir Richard Branson, Lord Sugar. All of these people started with pretty much nothing, but they had a dream, they had a goal, they had an inspiration, and they absolutely took action and they failed forward. There is something inside of us that is more powerful than we ever imagine, but it will only activate when we start to believe.

I spoke to somebody the other day and they said to me, "Oh my gosh, how do I get started, there are so many established people out there. I am never going to be as good as them". Let me tell you this, if you start to compare yourself to other people you have already lost the battle because you are not them, you are unique, you are you. You have a gift, and it is your power and your individuality and your strength, your courage, your confidence that determines where you are going to go in this life.

Minds2Wealth is about the ability to have a positive, engaged mind that says that everything is possible, that says that I can do it, that I have the power inside myself.

Now I can motivate you all day long, ladies and gentlemen, but the buck stops with you. I can write a book and it can help you or it can't. I can write a programme and it can help you or it can't. The only person that is going to benefit from my programme and my book is the person who is prepared to take action, the person who can graze their knees and get back up, graze their knees, and get back up and graze their knees and get back up again.

Because that makes you a warrior. That makes you battle hardened for what's in store for you because, ladies and gentlemen, it's not easy. This is the road less travelled. Welcome to Minds2Wealth ladies and gentlemen, a journey for champions, a journey for people who refuse to give up on life and on themselves, a journey for people who will stop at nothing to achieve success. Because very few people will achieve success in life. In fact, most people will fail because they doubt themselves and their ability and they will fail and that's the hardened truth. Perhaps five percent of people reading this book might take action.

Perhaps five percent of the people reading this book might have the courage and strength inside themselves to readjust themselves when they are feeling down, to find a way to slap themselves around the face when they find themselves being drawn to negative thoughts and comments and start talking about negative people.

Don't ever talk about the haters, don't ever talk about negative situations, don't ever talk about the people that you think are crazy, that are stamping all over positivity. Don't ever empower the conversation in your mind because you are a warrior that's on a mission and nothing and nobody can stop you unless you want it to.

And that is the difference between somebody who is going to move forward into my programme that I am going to help because I refused to give up, because I refused to stop. Because I refused to stop adjusting, changing, and improving. I refused not to improve myself, my life, my body, my mind, my fitness. I refused to give up on myself. It's up to you to refuse to give up on yourself.

Let me explain to you something very important, especially if you are after wealth creation. Your wealth will not grow until you have a wealthy mind. A wealthy and healthy mind comes before everything, because once you have got your mind right the wealth will come automatically.

Remember, if you chase money, Money always runs away from you, but if your mind is in tune and you are more relaxed and comfortable with yourself, guess what, the money comes to you. If you chase money, you lose it. If you chase your dreams, if you chase your ambition and chase the best version of yourself, without doubt, without fear, without procrastination a miracle happens; you start to make money with ease.

And that is why in this book we have spoken about bringing our minds together first in order for us to achieve our wealth because there is no point in having wealth without having a great mind.

Let me tell you something else about wealth. Wealth means different things to different people. Maybe wealth to you means to be a good human being, not everything is about money. It could be about you putting a smile on your face because somebody may have needed that this morning. A smile is wealth in itself, it is the inner wealth. Not everybody sees wealth as more money, it can mean more time to do the things you want to do, such as more meditation or more time enjoying the company of friends or family. What does wealth mean to you? Perhaps, for a football player it would be who could score more goals.

Some people have been lucky enough to fall over wealth and they have been lucky enough to make lots and lots of money, they have just fallen into an idea, and it has worked for them. Which is fabulous and they may have retained that wealth, which is beautiful, or Covid and the pandemic may have taken that away.

Whatever your circumstance, wherever you find yourself, you must remember that you have the power to change everything. You have the power to decide what you do every day; you have the power to decide what way your day is going to go. Whether you are going to wake up with the motivation and energy to take on the world.

Every single day you have the power to be a negative, miserable, depressing individual to be around. I was that person and I try every single day to remain positive. But let me tell you, I am only human and so are you. We are going to fall over in any minute, in any hour, in any day, in any week, in any month, in any year. We will fall over many times, and demons or our bad wolf can creep in at any time. How long you feed the bad wolf is up to you.

My advice is to remember that the good wolf is there, and the good wolf will fill you with energy, with positivity, with drive, with engagement. The good wolf will say to you, you're nearly there, keep going, keep moving forward, keep improving, don't ever be satisfied until you have found the perfect recipe, the printing machine to make money that's perfect for your life.

You could be a woman sitting at home, raising children, that is starting a business. You could be someone that is a barrister in London, and you have just woken up one day and you don't like your life and you are going to change your career. You may be somebody that is growing at a rate of knots, and you are not sure how to handle your money or what to do with your money.

Whatever your circumstances are, the Minds2Wealth programme has been built by a human being who has faced amazing challenges in his life. And I realised that the gift of my life, the challenge of my life, had to be put into writing. It had to be put into words because I know there are many people out there like me. And many of us don't feel that we want to change or need to change, but we know inside that something isn't quite right.

We know that we are not complete. And human beings, now more than ever before with this pandemic, want to feel complete. Because I believe that there has been the largest spiritual shift ever and I think we are moving into a brand-new world where people are saying to themselves perhaps the most important question of all: where do I belong in this world? What is my place? Where do I step into my genius? How do I truly feel beautiful inside and out every single day because I am doing what I love?

I have been trying to find my place in this world since that moment I had my bike accident. And ladies and gentlemen I am so pleased to tell you that I've arrived home.

This is Minds2Wealth and my name is Ali Shahraki and I look forward to working with you to help you find your genius to help you become awakened, to help you realise that the only person who can help you truly is you. I will be your guide, I will be there for you, I will share my energy, I will share my pain and I will share my love and my inspiration with you and from that you understand that my Rebirth Eye Model has been born. I will help you, but I can only help you if you're prepared to help yourself.

Don't look to me for the answers to your future. Don't look to me with "this course had better change my life Ali". Don't look to me to say I have invested in this course, and I hope it changes my life. Make a decision that you want to change, and my course will help you in that process but ultimately it is going to come down to you. Because even the best coaches can support and guide you but unless you get into that fight, unless you roll your sleeves up, unless you go knee deep in that mud, unless you go up to your neck in that pain when others won't, unless you are prepared to go into your mind and beyond the realms of what you think you know and what you don't know, you cannot possibly understand what you are going to know tomorrow.

Taking action and being accountable to yourself is the first step. I will help you fill in the blanks, but you are you, and only you are going to become that person that you could become if you have got the right mindset and determination. Work on yourself more than you work on your job because as Jim Rohn says.

Work harder on yourself than you do on your job. If you work hard on your job, you can make a living. If you work hard on yourself, you can make a fortune.

Jim Rohn

This is the reason I worked on myself more than my job. I spent the time when I was not working on my job working on myself instead of watching TV, going on Facebook etc. Success is not something that you can buy. Jim Rohn also says you have to attract success by becoming an attractive person. He says you have to become an attractive person. How? By learning a new language, learning a new skill. Working on your mind, sorting out your mindset. Success is not something that you pursue, it is what you attract by becoming attractive to the marketplace. And he was right. I had to learn more skills.

This doesn't mean you have to be good at everything yourself. Henry Ford famously responded in court when he was accused of being ignorant that with the push of a button, he could summon aid men who could answer ANY question he desired to ask concerning his business. He responded;

WHY I should clutter up my mind with general knowledge, for the purpose of being able to answer questions, when I have men around me who can supply any knowledge I require?

Henry Ford

The same goes for you, you may not have a row of buttons to summon people, but you do not have to know every answer yourself. I know you will be saying to yourself that when you first start something, you cannot afford to pay people. There is something to be said for knowing how things work because when you do build a team you will know the right questions to ask to make sure that you people you employ know their job. The other thing I have to say though is **leverage**! If you want someone to help you is there something that you have or that you can do that would help them in exchange for their assistance. Leverage is powerful. If someone says that is going to cost this amount I think, what can I give him in return.

First, you need to multiply your income, then you can triple it then you can time it by four, time it by five. But the first thing you have to do is work on yourself, you have to develop your skill first. You have to be a learner first then you can become the master. When I understood this, I started working on myself and I stopped being worried about making money and why the country doesn't have a good economy, why am I not making money, why are the wages going down? I started just working on myself and sharpening my axe helped me to move further forward.

So let me ask you a question as we end this book. Let me ask you just the one most important question, let me ask you the one, most powerful question that you are going to take away from this book, the most powerful feeling that is going to run through you, and only you will know the answer to this question. Here it comes ladies and gentlemen. Turn over to the nest page where the question is in bold. But before you do, before you answer that question, ask yourself, do you really want to know what you are letting yourself in for? Are you really ready to go knee deep in the pain of transition? Are you prepared to almost go through hell to come out the other side with everything you've always wanted?

What are you willing to do to achieve your goals and dreams, financially or none financially? How bad do you want it to happen for you too?

Turn over the page. Turn the page and answer the question.

What Is It That Is Stopping You From Moving Forward Today?

What is stopping you from moving your life and business forward today?

The answer should be nothing, if you've read this book and you believe that you can move forward then the answer should be nothing. However, at this point we would wish you the very best on your journey and we hope that you have enjoyed reading my book and that you have enjoyed reading and understanding a little about my own experiences in the hope that it will help you to move forward.

Visit www.minds2wealth.com To download your Wheel of life for free and assess your situation to find out what you can improve to shift your life.

I hope that my explanation of the Rebirth Eye Model has helped you as well. But for those who have still got an unanswered question, a burning desire to delve deeper and to move into my course then follow this link now and find out more about my signature Minds2Wealth programme where we will start to work together to fill in any of the blanks about where you are going.

www.Minds2Wealth.com

The only thing that you need to bring with you is the fact that you understand, and you feel that there is nothing that can stop you from moving forward. Everything else I will have the greatest pleasure to help you understand and to see and feel with clarity to help get you to the place you need to be.

With very best wishes,

Ali Shahraki

Creator Minds2Wealth

Founder ...

RESOURCES

Chapter 2

Dr Michael Beckwith on the four stages of spiritual awakening.

https://www.youtube.com/watch?v=vg-D2DMFbhk

The Story of Bamboo

https://www.youtube.com/watch?v=hLJFx_b2A2k

https://www.deangraziosi.com

Alice's Adventures in Wonderland by Lewis Carroll

Chapter 3

The story of the two wolves

https://en.wikipedia.org/wiki/Two_Wolves

Paulo Coelho, The Winner Stands Alone

https://www.goodreads.com/quotes/481819-life-has-many-ways-of-testing-a-person-s-will-either

Gibbs Reflective Cycle

https://www.ed.ac.uk/reflection/reflectors-toolkit/reflecting-on-experience/gibbs-reflective-cycle

Chapter 4

https://gentwenty.com/areas-of-personal-development/

You Were Born Rich by Bob Proctor

http://pardot.s3.amazonaws.com/marketing/You%20Were%20Born%20Rich%20Book.pdf

Chapter 5

https://www.brainyquote.com/quotes/abraham_lincoln_109275

Dr Michael Beckwith on the four stages of spiritual awakening.

https://www.youtube.com/watch?v=vg-D2DMFbhk

The story of Bamboo

https://www.youtube.com/watch?v=hLJFx_b2A2k

Chapter 10

Jim Rohn's Foundation for Success

https://www.success.com/jim-rohns-foundations-for-success/

Henry Ford Quotes

http://www.quoteswise.com/henry-ford-quotes-2.html

ABOUT THE AUTHOR

I am Ali Shahraki, (Lord Ali Shahraki)

-Senior Forex, Stock, Crypto, Gold, Silver, Oil trading and investing mentor and investor…

-Wealth creation & decision-making coach

-MBA Business Management

-ICF registered Life Coach

-Professional Investor

- NFT Creation & Investment Coach

- Father of young NFT & Metaverse Builder Kids and proud of them to be so forward compared to school education.

-Mindset Coach a super Dad to 4 Beautiful Kids, Only working with high performance and business people, help them to overcome their mental obstacle in their success journey. I also run mentoring programs in our company, School of Trading UK for people who are interested in investing and learning about stock market and forex. I am also joint venturist with investors all around the world, helping them to invest and grow their money.

In 2010, April the 10th ...

I had a bike crash which changed my life and made me to start a self-discovery journey to find myself and the path to success. I made my way up from being homeless in 2002 to be financially free in 2020. I learnt a lot through the journey.

I was Mr angry...and I always was blaming others for having pain and struggle in my life and that was up to 2010.In that accident, I died for around 17 minutes. You can call it whatever you want, but paramedic said there was no sign of life when they arrived 10 minutes after the crash and on his watch, I was out for 7 minutes before I came back.

I saw the event from outside my body. I had an out of body experience. That crash changed my life and the way I see life... changed my life and perspective. After that I made peace with my past and my death...

I was not scared of anything anymore from that point, because I faced my death. lost all my fears in life by facing my death. But there was and still is one fear in me, and that is something we call the fear of future regret. It is the fear that when I am older, looking back at my life, and see the things I did not try. It is the fear of not being able to say well done to myself for what I achieved in my life when I am at the end.

So, that is why I try anything in life to improve my life constantly and then try to influence others in a positive way too, and if it works then I keep doing it.

At the same time, I also reflect on my life every day, week, month, year and every 10 years to make sure I am doing everything I can to avoid that regret in the future.

I have never felt depressed or angry with situations since then. but I went on a journey of learning for the last 11 years to find out what happened to me.

I met many mentors, philosopher, religious leaders and even took training for a week in a temple of monks in Tibet to understand their views of the situation... and what happened to me.

Finally, dots were connected, after I finished my 3 years life coaching training with Robbins Madanes. Before that, I studied with mentors such as Richard Bandler, Joel Austin, John Butcher, Dr Michael Bernard Beckwith and many more mentors that I had in my journey of finding myself.

Now I live in the last hour of life because I do not know if I still be here or not within the next hour. I took being alive for granted for many years... instead of appreciating it.

Not anymore...

I don't take life for granted any more. I appreciate every moment of it. That accident made me to love life and only do the things I love. I learnt to forgive people quickly... and only live in a happy state, to create good memories for others.

Before the crash, I was angry at the whole world, blaming everyone for my downfalls and decisions...

Now, that I faced my death, I live to serve and help others in the moment that we live in. I live to create good memories for others, the one that are on my path and in my journey of life.

My mission is to affect a million people in a positive way while I am alive.

Getting a second chance was enough for me to change my life.

After 11 years of Deep Learning, self-development, reading many books in the subject of Money, wealth, and human behaviour and that is after many years of my university learning, I thought it is time to give back to people.

So, I created the Minds2Wealth program to help people following my path to a happier life. The aim is to help people in creating the road map they need to achieve what they want in life.

So, if you are lost, or been stuck behind obstacles on your way up in life or business, maybe you just need a lift to the next stage to improve your business or life! If that is you, then you should search Minds2wealth Or Ali Shahraki on any social media, look for our logo, and get in touch with us so we can help you complete your journey.

I am looking forward to helping you in this journey and the shift to the next stage

Best regards

Ali Shahraki

Don't Forget To add yourself to my Telegram, Discord & Facebook Group To Watch my podcast live and be notified of any Offers.

Discord: https://discord.gg/9D6TSJfy8F

Facebook: https://www.facebook.com/groups/moneyandinvestingtalk

Telegram: https://t.me/realalishahraki

Visit Our website www.minds2wealth.com To download Your Life assessment.

Printed in Great Britain
by Amazon

78620024R00098